Are you a

ROOKIE DAD?

When you engage your infant in the exercises presented in this one-of-a-kind parenting guide, you accomplish much more than you might know. Apart from the vitally important effects of bonding with your baby through fun time and play, these simple activities can also help *you* become more comfortable and capable in your new role. Discover pointers and coaching tips that will help you:

- deal with the stresses and demands a new baby brings
- keep sleepless nights—for father, mother, and child—to a minimum
- overcome the initial anxieties of holding a newborn
- keep Baby engaged while eating out, shopping, or traveling
- share parenting responsibilities with your partner
- make some leisure time for Dad, with no-stress exercises to do while watching the big game on TV!

Rookie Dad

Fun and Easy Exercises and Games for Dads and Babies in Their First Year

• • •

S U S A N   F O X

POCKET BOOKS

New York   London   Toronto   Sydney

An *Original* Publication of POCKET BOOKS

POCKET BOOKS, a division of Simon & Schuster, Inc.
1230 Avenue of the Americas, New York, NY 10020

Library of Congress Catalog-in-Publication Data

Fox, Susan.
   Rookie dad : fun and easy exercises and games for dads and babies
in their first year / Susan Fox.
      p. cm.
   Includes index.
   ISBN: 0-7434-1034-3
   1. Infants—Development—Miscellanea. 2. Father and infant—
Miscellanea. 3. Exercise for children. 4. Infants—Recreation I. Title.
HQ774.F68 2001
649'.122—dc21   00-140102

First Pocket Books trade paperback printing May 2001

10 9

POCKET and colophon are registered trademarks of
Simon & Schuster, Inc.

Book design by Lindgren/Fuller Design, Inc.

Cover design by Rod Hernandez
Front cover illustrations by Gary Johnson

Printed in the U.S.A.

To my sweetheart, my love forever

Contents

CONTENTS

Rookie Dad

CHAPTER ONE

The Pregame Show

"I'm pregnant!"

They're two of the most thrilling and frightening words in the English language, and your heart probably did a triple flip the first time you heard them. Odds are you still feel a little breathless when you think about the joy and excitement of having your first child, and about the huge responsibility of caring for the new human being who'll soon be calling you Dad.

Pregnancy is a joyous time, full of anticipation and wonderment. It's also a giant step into uncharted waters, so don't be surprised if you frequently wake up in the middle of the night with your mind full of classic dad-to-be worries: How will our life change when it's "we three" instead of "we two"? How will I support my child from diapers through college? Will my baby—and my partner—be healthy? Will I be a great dad, or a total jerk? Will I gross out when my partner's water breaks? Lose the car keys? Faint in the delivery room? If you talk with other

1

expectant dads you'll find that such sleepless nights and anxious moments are almost universal.

Another phenomenon that's almost universal is mood swings—and I'm not just talking about your significant other's. Granted, her hormones are doing somersaults, and she's laughing one minute and weepy or homicidal the next. But surprisingly, *your* hormones also change when your partner is pregnant: a recent study found that expectant fathers' levels of testosterone surge just before their babies arrive, and their levels of estrogen—a female hormone, normally scant in men—also skyrocket. And here's an even more remarkable fact: men whose partners are about to give birth also have elevated levels of prolactin, a hormone that plays a key role in breast-feeding. In addition, it's common for men to experience sympathetic pregnancy symptoms, ranging from nausea to weight gain—so you're not just kidding when you tell your friends, "We're pregnant!"

LET EVERYOnE KnOW: IT'S YOUR BABY, TOO

Even though you're an important player on the pregnancy team, you'll sometimes feel a little like a second-string benchwarmer. That's because right now, your partner is the center of attention. Her friends cluster around, asking how she feels, telling her she's radiant, throwing showers, bringing her little booties and teddy bears, and carting her off to shop for maternity clothes and baby gadgets. And every once in a while they remember to glance your way and ask—"You *do* know the route to the hospital, don't you?"

But don't let your friends and family convince you that you're little more than a sperm donor and a labor-day taxi driver. In the next chapter, I'll talk about studies showing just how important your job as Dad will be after your child arrives. Even before your baby is born, however, you're an equal partner in the parenting process—and you don't need to wear one of those pregnancy bellies to prove it. Your multiple roles during your partner's pregnancy include breadwinner, birthing coach, crib assembler, sympathetic shoulder, caretaker, swollen-foot massager, morale booster, and—frequently—saint. You're the one who has to reassure your partner that she's still beautiful, even as you're secretly wondering if those weird blue veins under her boobs will ever go away. You've probably been put in charge of everything from buying the car seat to setting up the college fund to painting the nursery. And, of course, you're the one making those late-night runs to the store for oysters, pickles, choco-brickle-ripple ice cream, and all the other foods your suddenly voracious partner craves at odd hours. Ever wonder what happened to the woman who used to say "I'm stuffed" after eating six pieces of popcorn?

In short, you'll play just as important a role in the pregnancy as your partner—and because you're sharing the work, it's important to share the joys as well. Take time to savor the traditional thrills of imminent fatherhood, including feeling your baby kicking and picking out fun toys. If you crave a more hands-on experience, take a few hours off work to visit the obstetrician with your partner, so you can hear your baby's heartbeat for the first time, or see Junior's first ultrasound picture. Take funny

3

pictures of your partner's big belly; she'll be more cooperative if you tell her she looks just like Demi Moore. Order your favorite childhood books from Amazon and start your own kid library with all the classics. And check out the expectant dads' groups on the Internet; they're full of advice and entertaining stories about the trials and joys of pregnancy, as seen from a man's point of view.

Many dads tell me the prospect of being a dad gave them an opportunity to review their own lives, and their relationships with their own parents. One expectant father spent several months compiling a book of his family's traditions, and he now shares the book with his child on holidays and special occasions. Another used a computer graphics program to create an illustrated book of favorite family stories, and still another—a genealogy buff—put together a book of family photos going back several generations.

The most important step you can take before your baby's birth, however, is to make sure you're knowledgeable about your new arrival. I know that many men's eyes glaze over at the sight of books about the birth process, but you'll feel more comfortable—and gain more respect from both your partner and her doctor—if you know what to expect as the pregnancy progresses. So pick up one of your partner's baby books and read a few pages each week about your baby's development. As you learn about what your little one is up to—sucking a thumb at twelve weeks, kicking and turning at sixteen weeks, dreaming at thirty-two weeks—you'll begin to feel a little like you're buddies already.

It's a must, too, to take a childbirth class with your partner. These classes take only a few evenings, and once you graduate, you'll be prepared for everything from the first labor pain to the first diaper. If possible, tour your hospital's obstetrics unit before your baby arrives, so you'll know your way around when D day arrives. And, of course, do one or two dry runs of the trip to the hospital, to make sure you know how long it takes to get there and the best route to take.

Still feeling a little nervous about how you'll do as a dad? Get some real-life experience by offering to baby-sit for a couple of hours for a friend who has a baby or young child. If you're nervous about the idea of being alone with a baby, then visit with other dads and play with their babies while the dads are on hand to offer pointers. Try changing a diaper and giving a bottle under their supervision, too.

Last but not least, take the time to get to know your baby, even before he or she is born. Remarkably, research shows that babies can hear and remember even when they're in the womb. In one study, researchers played the same music tapes or read the same stories to unborn babies for ten minutes every day. After the babies' birth, the researchers measured their sucking response to both the stories and music they'd heard before birth, and unfamiliar music and stories. Eighty-two percent of the babies were able to identify the music and stories they'd heard before they were born!

The moral of this research is that it's never too early to introduce yourself to your new son or daughter. The activities that follow will help you do just that, and enjoy a cuddle with your partner at the same time.

"Introducing Daddy"

- Put your hand on your partner's tummy.
- Tell your baby, "I'm your daddy. We're going to have fun playing games together. I'm going to keep you safe and protected."
- Place your head gently on your partner's tummy.
- Sing your favorite kid songs—"Take Me Out to the Ball Game," "Down at the Station," "The Wheels on the Bus," "I've Been Working on the Railroad," etc.

"Welcome Warm-Up"

- Warm your hands and coat them with lotion or baby oil.
- Gently massage your partner's tummy.
- See if you can find your baby's foot, head, and bottom while you massage and snuggle.

TIPS FOR WINNING

Is your relationship starting to seem decidedly unromantic as your house fills up with breast pumps, Lamaze manuals, and pamphlets full of drawings of your partner's innards? ("Notice the placenta forming at the left of the sketch . . .") Reignite the romance by coming home early one night with take-out Chinese and a bottle of sparkling cider. Light some candles, put on some nice music, and dance, even if anything more intimate is out of the question. You'll both enjoy the reminder that your partner is more than just a baby factory.

• • •

Talk to other dads. I know guys don't schmooze much about babies, but if you bring up the subject, your friends will be more than willing to share their experiences—and guys who've survived labor, delivery, and "oh-my-Lord-I'm-a-dad-now" stages can often offer reassuring advice.

• • •

There is only one, repeat one, correct answer to the question: "Do you still find me attractive?" If you say anything other than yes, you're dead meat—so resist the urge to be brutally honest, or even smart-alecky.

• • •

You've probably heard this already, but it's important: don't get mad at your partner if she says awful things during labor. If she calls you a swine, says she hates you, and threatens to break your arm if you ever get her pregnant again, just smile. You can tease her about it later—much later—but don't hold it against her, because the nicest

7

women say the darnedest things when they're dilated to eight centimeters.

THE SAFETY ZONE

Be sure that you're in charge of any painting, redecorating, and furniture-moving projects while your partner is pregnant. She shouldn't be breathing paint fumes or shoving heavy cribs or chairs around, so recruit some of your buddies to help you handle the nursery preparations.

• • •

If you have a cat, be sure to take over changing the cat litter. It's fine for a pregnant woman to cuddle, pet, and feed a cat, but contaminated cat litter can carry parasites that aren't healthy for your unborn child.

• • •

If you smoke, now's the time to quit—or at least to start going outdoors each time you light up.

• • •

Your partner can't drink for nine months, so show your support by limiting your own alcohol consumption.

• • •

From now on, your health is critically important to at least three people: you, your partner, and the child who'll be depending on you for years to come. So exercise regularly, cut down on the doughnuts, and get regular checkups.

SPECIAL PLAYS

As your baby's due date approaches, start saving your weekly copies of *Time, Newsweek,* or *U.S. News & World Report*. If you're really efficient, also save the daily newspaper that's published on the day he's born. Years from now, your child will be fascinated when he reads about what went on in the world right before, during, and just after his arrival.

• • •

Now is a good time to start talking about some of those major parenting decisions. What kind of religious training, if any, do you want your child to have? Do you think it's okay to watch raunchy TV shows around kids? Should swearing around your children be taboo? Should your kids call your dad's third partner "Grandma," or save that for their biological grandmothers? There's no end to the fascinating questions that arise during parenthood, and the more of these questions you resolve ahead of time, the easier your job will be later on.

• • •

Start a dad journal. Write down funny stories—one dad, for instance, wrote about how the nurses in his partner's birthing room were so busy watching the finale of *Dallas* that they almost missed the delivery! Stick in photos of you and your pregnant partner, or a table napkin from the restaurant where you went to celebrate when the pregnancy test came out positive. Years from now, when your middle-aged memory gets a little spotty, you'll enjoy these reminders of your days as a dad-to-be.

ADVICE FROM THE COACH

I hate blood and messes, and while everyone else in our Lamaze class was oohing and aahing over the birth movie, I got sick to my stomach. I'm worried about how I'll hold up in the delivery room.

Guess what: every other guy who watched that film in your Lamaze class is secretly worrying about the same thing. However, labor day is such an action-packed event—rushing to the hospital, throwing on your scrubs, panting with your partner during labor—that you probably won't have time to think about fainting. And every dad I've ever talked to, even those who'd dreaded being in the delivery room, said the experience was priceless. So don't worry: while characters in TV comedies are forever passing out at the sight of a woman giving birth, it doesn't happen much in real life, and the joy of the experience is worth the tiny risk of winding up passed out cold on the delivery room floor.

My partner had a gorgeous figure before she got pregnant, but now she's huge. I hate to sound shallow, but I'm worried about what she'll look like after the baby's born. Am I being a jerk?

No, you're just being a guy. Men take their partners' appearance seriously, and it's natural for them to worry about pregnancy pounds—particularly since many women do have difficulty losing the weight they put on when they're expecting. However, rather than fretting about your partner's poundage, plan positive ways to help her when she wants to get back in shape after the birth.

But what if your partner still puts on a few pounds? My advice: be philosophical. In the coming years, your hairline will recede, you'll get some wrinkles, and you'll probably put on a little spare tire yourself. As your marriage and family become increasingly important, you'll pay less attention to superficial appearances—and now is a good time to start.

One more note: don't push your partner to watch her weight while she's pregnant. Right now, those extra pounds aren't a problem. In fact, the *opposite* is true: women who gain too few pounds during pregnancy can put their children at risk for developmental problems. So tell your partner she looks beautiful and healthy, because it's true.

My partner wants me to cut the cord after our baby is born. I'm not sure I can face this.

Talk it over and see how strongly she feels about this. If it's not a big deal, let the doctor do it. If she thinks it's important, then you'll earn lots of points for one quick chore that's not anywhere near as gross as it sounds. One dad told me, "I just pretended I was cutting a big piece of spaghetti."

We're adopting a baby. It seems strange to miss out on the pregnancy stage—will I feel the same about my baby as I would if I'd seen her being born?

Virtually all adoptive fathers say they felt the same intense feelings of joy and protectiveness when they first held their adopted babies as they would have if they'd cut the cord themselves. And, in many ways, the adoption process is like a pregnancy: the long wait, the anxiety, the "will our baby be all right?" worries. So while you may miss out on morning sickness and breaking water, you'll feel every bit as relieved and excited when your baby is finally placed in your arms.

DAD'S PREDELIVERY SCORECARD

- You and your partner have a birth plan (*what to do, where to go, who to call, what to take*).
- You've packed the bag of supplies to take to the hospital, and you know where it is.
- You have a list of phone numbers of people to call, including the doctor, the hospital, and the relatives.
- The car seat is installed and ready for the trip home from the hospital.
- You've bought your partner a gift to present after the baby is born and hidden it safely away. (My recommendation: a locket to hold a picture of your newborn baby.)

CHAPTER TWO

Game Time

Exercises from Birth to Three Months

Way to go—you're a dad! But don't you wish this game came with a rule book?

It doesn't, but don't panic—you'll do fine. And don't worry if you're not an instant expert at feeding, diapering, or burping your baby. Every new player in the "dad game" is all thumbs at first, and a few fumbles are inevitable. Just try not to fumble the baby!

It's also par for the course to feel both left out and stressed-out at this stage. Everybody's fussing over your partner and goo-gooing at your baby, while you've been relegated to fetching diapers and doing dishes. There's a constant parade of relatives, neighbors, and friends through your living room. There's that new aroma of wet diapers, sour milk, and poop pervading your entire home. And as for a good night's sleep, decent meals, or sex, forget it—at least for a while. By the time your first month of life as a dad is over, you'll be on a first-name basis with every fast-food owner in town, you'll feel like a monk, and you'll truly understand the meaning of the term sleep deprivation.

You'll quickly find, however, that the joys of your new job as a dad far outweigh the minor inconveniences. No other sensation can compare to the warm, fuzzy feeling you get when your baby looks at you, or the realization that a part of you will live on forever in a new generation. You're probably surprised at how protective you feel toward your baby, and how you're already looking forward to introducing your new son or daughter to football, Disneyland, and pizza. You're in for the biggest adventure of your life, and you'll enjoy almost every minute of it.

At the same time, it's natural to be nervous—"Am I holding her right?" "Will I drop her?" "What did she just do all over the front of my shirt?" It takes a little while to

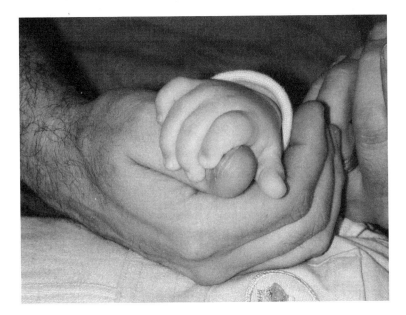

get used to this stranger in your midst, especially since it's a pretty demanding little stranger. And you two still have a lot to learn about each other.

How do you begin to form a relationship with this tiny, mysterious being who's taken over your life? Baby books are full of intimidating advice about bonding and nurturing, but it's actually simple. Put on an old pair of jeans, get down on the floor with your baby, and goof around together. Talk to your baby. Get up for that 2 A.M. feeding once in a while. Learn how to change a diaper, coax a burp, and make those entertaining raspberry noises on your baby's tummy. It doesn't take a degree in psychology to become friends with a one-month-old. It just takes some time, a little effort, and the ability to laugh when your baby barfs all over your favorite sweatshirt.

THE IMPORTANCE OF BEING DAD

While you're getting to know your new arrival, you can be giving her a head start in life. The exercises in this book, while they're easy and fun, are actually designed to work on your baby's developmental skills—everything from hand-eye coordination and muscle tone to balance, agility, and even memory and thinking skills. If you want to give your son or daughter an advantage on the playing field or in the classroom, now's the time to begin.

In addition, if you start working out with your baby now, you'll be a role model right from the beginning. That's important, because fathers play a crucial role in helping their children succeed in life. According to the

National Center for Education Statistics, children of involved fathers are more likely to get A's, enjoy school, and participate in extracurricular activities, and less likely to need to repeat a grade, than children of uninvolved dads. Moreover, a recent study in the journal *Pediatrics* found that children whose fathers participate in their upbringing are more likely than other children to be economically self-sufficient and have healthy lifestyles. And research by psychology professor Richard Koestner and colleagues found that children of fathers who regularly spend time with their kids are more compassionate than children of fathers who don't.

In addition, boys who spend time with their dads and have a close relationship with them develop sportsmanship and other winning skills. As Tiger Woods said when he won the PGA Championship for the first time in 1999, "My dad was my greatest support." And the rewards of being a good dad are immeasurable. Just look at the photos of Mark McGwire hugging his dad after that record-breaking home run.

Dads are just as vital to their daughters' success. According to a report by the Department of Health and Human Services, girls who are close to their fathers are more likely than other girls to get high grades.[1] Girls who have solid relationships with their fathers feel more competent in math and are more secure in their femininity; conversely, research shows that girls raised in households without fathers are likely to have lower self-esteem, and to

---

[1.] "HHS Fatherhood Initiative," Health and Human Services fact sheet, June 19, 1999.

have difficulty forming healthy romantic relationships.[2] Dozens of successful sports figures, from tennis star Chris Evert to softball gold medalist Lisa Fernandez, say their fathers inspired them to become athletes.

In fact, children of both sexes are more successful in almost every area of life if they have supportive, "hands-on" dads. According to the Health and Human Services report, girls and boys with actively involved fathers are only half as likely as other children to drop out of high school or end up in jail, and only a quarter as likely to need help for emotional or behavioral problems, including teen pregnancy, drinking, and drug abuse.

Scientists also tell us that dads contribute to infants' early development in ways that mothers don't. For instance, Yale professor Kyle Pruett notes, "Men encourage their babies' curiosity and, more specifically, encourage them actively to solve physical and intellectual challenges." While moms tend to pick comfortable activities that they know their babies can master, dads like to expand their babies' horizons by nudging them to learn new skills and experience new adventures.

In short, you're important to your baby from day one. Along with your baby's mom, you're the Most Valuable Player in the real-life game of raising a moral, intelligent, happy, self-confident, and healthy child. Luckily, at this stage in the game, that job is simple.

So set aside just a few minutes a day, put on your old clothes, get on the floor, and play with your baby. You'll

---

[2] "Father Presence Matters: A Review of the Literature," Deborah J. Johnson, report of the National Center on Fathers and Families, 1999.

start building a good relationship, and help your infant grow and learn and explore. And years from now, if your daughter wins that gold medal, or your son catches the winning pass at the homecoming game, you can say—"I helped my kid do that!".

"Daddy Huddle"

Birth to Three Months

Okay, guys, it can't get any easier than this. Surprisingly, however, this really *is* an exercise. It teaches your baby to lift her head and keep it centered—important for promoting balance and good body alignment.

- Find a good game on TV.
- Sit on a chair, lounger, or sofa to watch it.
- Place your baby on your shoulder and encourage her to snuggle into your neck and shoulder. Be sure her head is straight and not turned to one side, and her arms are close to her body.

- While you're watching TV together, talk to your baby about the game. Now is a perfect time to explain the intricacies of offensive formations in football, or back-door plays in basketball, or the forward crisscross in hockey—because, for this brief moment in your relationship, your child may actually believe you know what you're talking about.

GAME TIP: *At this age, your baby is forming sensory patterns that tell her how to move and position her body. Holding her in good alignment now will help her sit up straight, crawl well, walk well, and have good posture later.*

"nose to nose"

One Week to Three Months

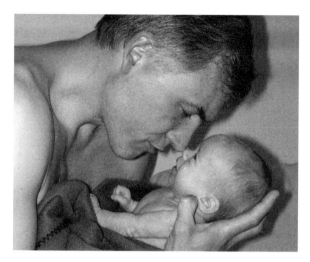

This exercise helps your baby learn to focus and track objects. It also helps her learn "optical righting," the skill of turning her head to look at an object.

- Cradle your baby with one hand.
- With your other hand, place your baby's hands against your cheeks.
- Enjoy looking at each other.
- Encourage your baby to focus by speaking softly to your baby when she's looking at you.

GAME TIP: *Babies learn to focus their eyes sometime between four and eight weeks, and learn to track—that is, to follow moving objects with their eyes—between eight and twelve weeks.*

"Meet the Coach"

Birth to Three Months

This simple activity promotes fine motor coordination and helps your baby learn to feel safe and secure with you.

- Lie on the carpet or a soft blanket, facing your baby.
- Open your baby's fist, moving her thumb outside her fingers. Gently stroke her hand, moving from the fingers to the wrist.
- Place your finger into your baby's hand and let your baby hold it.

GAME TIP: *A newborn baby has an involuntary grasp reflex. This exercise helps her learn to keep her hands more opened, and allows her to become accustomed to touch.*

"Game Face"

Birth to One Month

This exercise helps your baby learn to keep her head centered and stable—a skill she'll need soon, when she learns to sit up. It also promotes shoulder stability, teaches your baby not to be startled when you touch her, and helps her learn to use her eyes together to focus. In addition, it gives her practice in keeping her arms forward in preparation for reaching for objects.

- Lie your baby on your lap, faceup, with her hips and knees bent. Your baby's feet will be closest to you, with her head closer to your knees.
- Cradle your baby's head, shoulders, and arms in your own arms. Her head should be centered, with her chin

touching her chest. Her arms should be forward, in front of her shoulders.

- Keep your baby's bottom up, with her feet touching your chest.
- Slowly move your legs from side to side about one inch at a time while making entertaining faces at your baby. Come back to the center each time. If your baby looks or smiles at you, respond by saying her name and "Hi!"

GAME TIP: *When you shift your baby from side to side in this exercise, you'll be stimulating her vestibular system—the inner-ear system that tells her that she's moving, and in what direction. It'll be important later, in helping her to balance and preventing her from falling.*

"Flying High with Dad"

Birth to Two Months

This exercise works on balance and equilibrium, and helps your baby learn to keep her neck and back in alignment and her head centered. It also helps her learn to pay attention to you—a skill you'll appreciate in years to come! In addition, this game helps your baby become accustomed to gentle movement without startling her, teaches her that it's fun to move in space, and works on optical righting, a skill in which your baby's eyes and head work together.

- Hold your baby as shown in the photo, with one hand behind her head and the other supporting her bottom.

- Gently lift your baby in an arc, and then slowly bring
her back to your chest. As you bring your baby up to
your face, stop and encourage her to look at you.
Repeat, being careful to move slowly and smoothly.

GAME TIP: *Keep your baby's head higher than her bottom throughout this exercise. Also, lift your baby slowly to avoid frightening her. Newborn babies are very sensitive to gravity because they lack the muscle control required to compensate.*

"Crunch Time"

Birth to One Month

Helps your baby learn to balance and experience the sensation of moving in space. Helps you develop killer abs.

- Lie on your back on your sofa.
- Place your baby on your chest, with her face on your shoulder. Be sure she's on the shoulder facing the back of the sofa, so there's no danger of her rolling off onto the floor when you do this exercise. Be very careful to support her on both sides, so she can't fall.
- Do crunch sit-ups while holding your baby. Support her head, and don't press too hard on her with your hands.
- Between crunches, stroke your baby's back from her neck to her bottom, to encourage her to lift her head.

GAME TIP: *When you move your baby from a horizontal to a partially vertical position during this exercise, she'll be experiencing the sensation of using her body against gravity. As she learns to lift her head and neck, and begins to push up with her forearms and hands, she'll build the shoulder stability and strength she'll need later to crawl, reach, and hold toys.*

"Team Talk"

Birth to Three Months

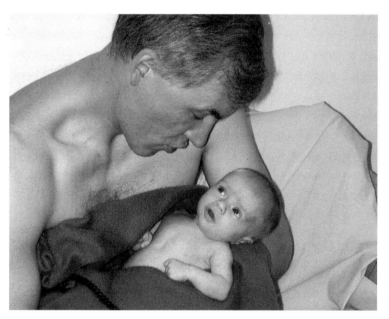

As you talk to your baby, she'll begin to recognize the sound of your voice and turn toward you. In addition, you'll be teaching her early listening skills.

- Hold your baby on your lap.
- Talk to your baby. When she looks at you, say, "Hi, Hannah."
- Sing songs to your baby over and over again.

GAME TIP: *Vary your tone and the loudness of your voice so your baby can experience a variety of sounds.*

TIPS FOR WINNING

Newborn babies are easily startled when you move them. When you pick your baby up or put her down, her arms and head may fly backward behind her shoulders, frightening her. To avoid this startle reflex, first touch your baby firmly and wait a few seconds while she becomes accustomed to your touch. Then support her head with one hand and cradle her shoulders with the other hand as you move her. Also, try not to push or pull on her arms or legs when you're diapering, dressing, or lifting her.

• • •

Bring home flowers.

• • •

The first few times you leave the baby with a relative or a sitter, don't be surprised if your partner is nervous. Let her call home every fifteen minutes, and don't tease her about it.

• • •

In fact, don't tease her about much of anything. Remember, her hormones are a little whacked-out right now, so her sense of humor may have gone into hiding.

• • •

Even if your partner is nursing, offer to give your baby a bottle once in a while. It won't interfere with nursing the baby, and it'll give you an opportunity to enjoy the cozy intimacy of feeding time. If you introduce both the bottle and the breast within the first month, nipple confusion—in which a baby accustomed to the breast won't take a bottle, or vice versa—is almost never a problem.

Tell your partner she's beautiful every chance you get, *especially* when she's in that "I'll-never-look-like-a-human-being-again" mood. And don't tell her that she smells like baby puke, even though she does.

• • •

You'll all feel better if the household chaos is partially under control, so do your own chores without being reminded, and surprise your partner by doing a few of hers, too. But set realistic goals for tidiness, because your house won't look neat for a long, *long* time.

• • •

Watch the baby for an hour or two every day, so your partner can take a nap.

• • •

Does your baby wake up and scream when you move her into or out of the car? Maybe you should get a car seat that converts to a stroller. You'll be able to move your sleeping baby from stroller to car seat and back to stroller without disturbing a nap.

• • •

Don't feel silly if you talk baby talk to your baby. Studies show that babies who are talked to or sung to in a high-pitched voice, and whose parents use short, repetitive syllables, will learn words more readily later on.

THE SAFETY ZONE

Always move your baby gently, and support her head securely.

. . .

Make sure the slats on your baby's crib are no farther than two and three-eighths inches apart. If you're using a secondhand crib, check the slats to be sure that they're still sturdy. And whether your crib is new or used, check the Internet to make sure there are no recall notices posted for it. You can also use the Net to check for recalls on high chairs, playpens, car seats, and toys.

. . .

Now you have an extra reason to check your smoke detector batteries regularly—and, if you have gas appliances, to buy a carbon monoxide detector. Also buy plenty of night-lights, so you'll be less likely to trip while you're carrying your baby through the house for one of her late-night feedings.

. . .

Remember the no-strings-attached rule: avoid dressing your baby in hats or jackets with cords long enough to create a strangling hazard, and buy bibs that fasten with Velcro or snaps rather than strings. Also, use a pacifier clip rather than putting your baby's pacifier on a ribbon.

. . .

Use a head support in your newborn baby's car seat, and make sure it's adjusted correctly. Provide additional support for very young babies or preemies by using a car seat insert.

SPECIAL PLAYS

Gently rock, swing, or dance with your baby. Infants love to move, and you'll be teaching your baby how it feels to move in space.

• • •

Mail call is a good opportunity for quality time. Cuddle your baby in your rocking chair or La-Z-Boy while you sort through your letters; she'll love snuggling against your warm chest, and that precious bundle will make you feel more philosophical when you open that massive Visa bill for the crib, the stroller, the car seat, the bassinet, the baby swing, the gross of Pampers. . . .

• • •

Hum songs while your baby is resting on your shoulder. She'll enjoy the vibration and the sound.

ADVICE FROM THE COACH

My partner seems exhausted. She doesn't ask me about my day. I miss the way it was before the baby. When will she get back to being normal?

Your partner seems exhausted because she *is* exhausted, and that won't change for several months. Be patient! First, she's suffering from sleep deprivation—a problem you can help solve by getting up at least two or three times a week for those middle-of-the-night feedings. Second, she's learning how to juggle her usual workload with the added job of caring for a totally dependent person. If she's taking time off from work, she's also suffering from "role shock"—that change from being a career woman to being a poop scrubber and milk machine. And last but definitely not least, your partner's hormone levels, which soared during pregnancy, have crashed like a bad Indy driver. They'll get back to normal in a few months, but meanwhile, she's going to be fatigued, a little "blue," and likely to bite your head off on a regular basis.

The solution? Take over more of the baby care, do more of the housework, and resign yourself to the fact that this is a time in your life where your needs don't come first—or even second. This, too, shall pass, and in the meantime you have a chance to be a hero for putting up with it.

One important note. If your partner's blues turn into serious, chronic sadness or fatigue, or her behavior changes to the degree that it alarms you, get her to a doctor. She could be suffering from postpartum depression (PPD), a potentially dangerous condition that affects 10 to 15 percent of new mothers. PPD generally starts as a bout of the blues but develops into severe depression, anxiety, and sometimes even rejection of the baby. Additional symptoms can include loss of appetite, sleeplessness, confusion, memory loss, excessive concern or lack of concern for the baby, panic attacks, feelings of hopelessness or inadequacy, or fear of harming the baby. Unlike the blues, PPD doesn't clear up on its own but persists for months. Luckily, the condition can be treated quickly and effectively with hormones or antidepressants, so there's no reason to hesitate if you suspect that your partner is suffering from PPD.

What about sex?

Get serious. Your partner just passed a bowling ball. She's tired, she's sore, she's dripping milk, her boobs hurt, her back hurts, her stomach is nothing but flab, and she probably has stitches in a very sensitive area. Even if she *could* have sex she wouldn't want to, so you're going to be celibate for six weeks or so. Grin and bear it, and do whatever you used to do when you were fifteen.

Even when you *do* have sex again, be prepared for things to be a little different. That's because your partner's body has changed—literally from head to toe, and all points in between. You may feel a little like you're having sex with a stranger, but you'll get used to the difference. In fact you'll be so desperate by then, you might not even notice.

I'm overwhelmed when I think about the financial responsibilities I'll be dealing with, now that I'm a dad—and to make matters worse, my partner is making noises about not returning to work.

Having a baby is a life-changing event, and many women who loved their jobs find it a challenge to return to the office after their maternity leave ends. If money is tight, see if you can come up with a creative solution. For instance, your partner might be able to work part-time at a home business, or her boss might let her "telecommute" via computer instead of going in to her job every day. Or, if she's concerned about leaving your baby with strangers, perhaps you and she can work staggered shifts, so one of you can be home with the baby all of the time.

I want to play golf on Saturday afternoons, just like I did before the baby was born, but I feel guilty about leaving my partner home to cope with the house and the baby. Will I ever be able to enjoy my weekends again?

For the first month or two, your partner will need you on duty every weekend. Eventually, however, you will be able to take turns getting out on weekends or evenings, and someday you'll even get brave enough to hire a sitter. You might not work in eighteen holes as often as you'd like over the next few years, but don't sell your clubs—you'll be back on the green slicing drives again someday soon. In the meantime, focus on recreational activities you and your partner can enjoy at home in your fleeting moments of peace—even if it's just renting videos and making popcorn.

My partner and I had a huge argument over whether or not our son should be circumcised. She won, but I'm still upset because I think we made the wrong decision.

It won't be the last time you feel that way! One of the toughest aspects of parenting is that two loving, intelligent people, whose sole goal is to raise a happy, healthy child, will frequently disagree about just how to do that. Also, if family life is new to you and your partner, and you've each spent years as independent adults, it can be difficult to learn the art of compromising and negotiating.

When your disagreements are minor—"When should we tell our child that Santa Claus isn't real?"—you'll usually be able to resolve them easily. But over the next twenty years, you'll face plenty of Big Questions: "Should our baby be circumcised?" "Should we let our ten-year-old go on a camping trip with a scoutmaster we don't know?" "What do we do if we find beer/marijuana joints/birth control pills/condoms in our teen's room?" Often, there are no right or wrong answers to these issues. The best advice I can offer is to discuss the issues calmly as a team rather than flying off the handle, and to listen to your partner's views with an open mind, while expecting the same open-mindedness from her. Usually, if you can just keep talking, you'll come to a decision you can both live with. If not, ask the people you trust—a priest or rabbi, your family doctor, a wise grandparent—for advice.

CHAPTER THREE

Touchdown: Getting Your Baby to Sleep

Exercises from Birth to Four Months

In six hours, you're making the biggest presentation of your life.

You have to be psyched. You have to be amazing. You have to be brilliant. And none of this matters *at all* to the purple-faced baby who's screaming inconsolably on your shoulder as you pace the living room floor, watching the clock tick past 2 A.M.

It's amazing how long a baby can stay awake—and what's more amazing, as you're no doubt discovering, is how your baby always resists sleep the most insistently on the nights when you *really, really* need your rest.

TIPS FOR COPING WITH AN INSOMNIAC BABY

When you first imagined evenings with your new baby, back before reality set in, you probably pictured yourself sitting on the sofa beaming paternally as your partner rocked your cherub peacefully to sleep. And, in fact, this touching scene probably occurs fairly often at your house. Unfortunately, it's likely to be followed by another scene, in which that same innocent babe you gently tucked into bed at eight o'clock is transformed, somewhere between midnight and 3 A.M., into a shrieking ball of fury.

It's important to realize, however, that your baby doesn't *want* to drive you crazy—really. To understand why he can't sleep, consider the world from his point of view. First, he has a very small tummy and he wakes up starving in the middle of the night. And at this stage, a big, dark, cold crib seems like a pretty lonely place. Think of how a motel in a strange town feels to you when you're on the road; to your baby, that dark crib feels just as impersonal. In contrast, a big, hairy dad chest feels warm and cozy and familiar. In addition, your baby frequently pees up a storm sometime during the night, and there's nothing like a wet, cold diaper to make sleeping impossible.

The good news is that your baby's waking-up-in-the-middle-of-the-night stage is usually temporary, although by "temporary" I mean that you'll probably get a good night's sleep sometime within the next year. Within three months if you're really lucky. The bad news is that in the meantime, you'll discover that the dead of night is all too lively when there's a new baby around the house. It's unusual, at least in the beginning, for an infant to sleep more than three hours at a stretch.

Fortunately, there are some good tricks for coaxing even the fussiest baby back to sleep. They don't always work—nothing does—but they'll at least improve your odds. Here, in no particular order, are the best ways to convince your night owl that it's bedtime.

- *Start a routine.* We're all creatures of habit, and babies are no exception. If you start a bedtime ritual early on, your son or daughter will eventually associate this ritual with getting sleepy. At about the same time each night, schedule a warm bath and a bedtime story afterward. Shortly before bedtime, give your baby a bottle, so his stomach will be comfortably full. Turn off the TV, and play soothing music. Sing the same bedtime songs each night.
- *Give your baby a rubdown.* A slow, gentle massage, starting at your baby's head and shoulders and working all the way down to the toes, will make his muscles relax and work out tension. After bath time, use baby's towel to give him a gentle rubdown.
- *Movement helps.* Buy a good, sturdy rocking chair and try rocking your baby to sleep. If rocking fails, place him in his swing, making sure his head is supported. Or put him in his stroller or a backpack, and take a walk together—either around the house or, weather permitting, outside.
- *If that doesn't work, go for a drive.* It's a strange fact that lots of babies who won't sleep a wink when they're placed in bed will doze off happily in a car seat while dad cruises the neighborhood blasting Metallica on the radio. Of course, keeping your baby asleep when you

move him from the car to the house is a challenge. To make it easier, put a blanket in the car seat so you can keep him snug while you transfer him.

- *Take a relaxing bath with your baby.* Cradled in your arms in the tub, he'll feel warm, secure, and if you're lucky, drowsy.
- *Swaddle your baby and place him in a bassinet rather than in his crib.* Many babies are more comfortable when they're snugly wrapped and placed in a small bed rather than a big crib.
- *Play a tape of womb sounds.* It may not be your idea of music, but babies love it. You can buy a tape at almost any baby store.
- *Warm your baby's clothes and blanket in the dryer before you dress him.* If it's chilly, warm his bed with a covered hot water bottle before you tuck him in, being sure to remove it before putting your baby in the crib.

Sometimes, unfortunately, none of these techniques will work. If you've given it your best shot and your baby is still screaming, simply put him to bed, shut the door, go out in the backyard, and read a good book or have a beer. Eventually, when he has worn himself out, your baby will fall asleep. And believe it or not, the neighbors won't think you're beating or neglecting your child. In fact, they'll probably be laughing their heads off—because most of them have been through the screaming-baby stage themselves.

You should also find a capable sitter early on, so you and your partner can take occasional breaks—especially if you're dealing with a colicky baby who fusses day and night. It's important to realize how stressed-out you can become while listening to a screaming baby, especially if you're sleep-deprived yourself. You're biologically wired to respond emotionally to the cries of your baby, which means that all that crying upsets you a lot more than it upsets your newborn.

In addition to the tips I've outlined, the following activities can put your baby in the right frame of mind to fall asleep. They're specially designed to help your baby relax in preparation for naptime or bedtime.

"Short Strokes"

Birth to Two Months

A newborn baby's fingers are as important as his eyes and ears in exploring his universe. In this activity, you'll introduce your baby to new textures, and help him get better acquainted with you as well, through his sense of touch. In addition, this relaxing game will calm your baby and help prepare him for nap time.

- Place your baby, lying on his side, on a bop cushion. If you don't have a bop, place him on a soft blanket, supporting his back against a pillow or sofa back so he doesn't fall backward.

- Next, lying face-to-face with your baby, introduce him to new textures, one at a time. Let him feel daddy's fleece sweatshirt, a terry cloth towel, a vinyl jacket, a smooth plastic toy, or a bumpy lemon. Give him time to explore and enjoy each object.
- Let your baby feel your hands, fingers, and ears, touch your face stubble, and feel the hair on your head and arms.

GAME TIP: *When possible, do this and other bedtime activities with the lights dimmed or turned off. Your baby's body will produce more melatonin—a chemical that naturally induces sleep—when it's dark.*

"Groomed for Success"

Birth to Six Months

Here's a fun exercise—but only for babies who have enough hair! It promotes visual focusing, decreases your baby's startle reflex, and helps him learn to keep his head centered and his arms forward.

- Place your baby on his back, on a bed or sofa or on your lap.
- Gently lift your baby's legs so they're supported by your chest, as shown.
- Provide support as needed, to keep your baby's head centered.
- Brush your baby's hair, looking into his eyes as you do.

GAME TIP: *Be sure to use a small, soft, baby hairbrush. Also, gently massage your baby's hair before starting, so he won't be startled by the feel of the brush.*

"Eyes on the Ball"

Birth to Six Weeks

Designed for the budding football or basketball player, this exercise helps promote your baby's ability to look at and follow objects with both eyes, and to keep his head centered. It also helps develop a straight back and teaches your baby to reach forward.

- Put your baby on his side, on a soft blanket.
- Lie next to your baby, facing him.
- Roll a soft cloth ball, a Nerf football, or a basketball—preferably a red, orange, or black-and-white patterned ball—along the blanket between you and your baby, or hold a ball on a string where he can reach it. This is more entertaining if you make goofy noises.
- Let your baby touch the ball when it's close to him. Help him to look at the ball and follow its movements by swinging it slowly from side to side. Stop moving

the ball if your baby stops looking at it, and help him refocus before you move it again.

• Gradually lift the ball and encourage your baby to reach forward and touch it.

GAME TIP: *A newborn can't differentiate colors, but he can tell the difference between dark and light. He'll be able to recognize different colors when he's about two months old.*

"Flashlight Tag"

Birth to Three Months

This activity will help your baby develop eye-tracking skills—which he'll need later to catch a pass or hit a home run—while relaxing and soothing him in preparation for sleep. You'll need a flashlight.

- Put your baby on his side on a sofa, a bed, or your lap, with a thin quilt or blanket underneath him. Turn off the lights.
- Turn on the flashlight and move the beam around the room while singing or talking quietly to your baby. Move the flashlight beam slowly, naming your baby's toys and stuffed animals as you shine the light on them.

GAME TIP: *If your baby is over two months old, try using a flashlight with different colored bulbs.*

"Take a Swing"

Birth to Three Months

If you're still a little insecure about holding your baby, you can do this exercise with your baby in a front pack or an infant carrier.

- Dress your baby comfortably for bed—see game tip below.
- Hold your baby as shown and swing him *very slowly and gently* from side to side, with one hand supporting his head and neck as shown, while the other supports his bottom. Be sure you have a good grip, and be careful not to let your baby's head fall backward.

- Let your baby watch your face as you do this exercise. Talk or sing to him while he's swinging.

GAME TIP: *One guaranteed way to create a cranky, sleepless baby is to dress him either too lightly or too warmly. If it's cool— or if your baby is a preemie and not well padded—be sure to dress him snugly in warm clothes. In warm or hot weather, however, stick with just a diaper.*

"Hammock Halftime"

Birth to Two Months

There's nothing like a swing in a hammock to make a person—big or small—think about snoozing. A swing in a real hammock with dad is great, but if you don't have one, a blanket makes a good substitute. In addition to being restful, this exercise will help your baby learn head control.

- Place a blanket (three by four feet, or larger) on the floor, and fold the sides of the blanket into the middle.
- Place your baby snugly in the center of the blanket.
- Gather the blanket at the top and bottom ends, at your baby's head and feet, creating a hammock.

- Lift the blanket at both ends, keeping your baby's head forward and his arms and legs inside the blanket.
- Holding the ends of the blanket, gently rock your baby forward and backward and/or side to side.

GAME TIP: *To make your baby even more cozy, warm the blanket in the dryer before you do this activity. When your baby falls asleep, use the blanket to ease him into his crib without waking him up.*

"Relaxing Rubdown"

Birth to Two Months

Here's another exercise that can help your baby relax.

- Put your baby across your lap or on a bop cushion, resting on his tummy.
- Gently rub his back, working from his neck to his bottom. Give him occasional pats, as if you're burping him.

GAME TIP: *If you have rough hands, use some baby lotion. Be sure to rub your hands together first, to warm up the lotion.*

TIPS FOR WINNING

Sucking helps your baby relax and might encourage him to doze off. Give him a pacifier, or let him suck on your little finger. Be sure your hands are clean, your fingernails are too short to scratch his mouth, and your finger is nail-side down.

• • •

Hum or sing to your baby while you're rocking him to sleep.

• • •

Often babies who refuse to nap during the day will doze off after five or ten minutes in a baby swing. Buy a battery-powered swing; it's a little more expensive than a wind-up swing, but it's worth it.

• • •

Purchase a dimmer switch for your baby's room. Many babies fall asleep more easily when there's a light on, and a dimmer switch will allow you to turn off the light sneakily.

• • •

Avoid giving your baby a bottle of milk when you put him in his crib, because it can rot his teeth. Of course, your baby doesn't have any teeth at first—but you don't want to start a bad habit.

THE SAFETY ZONE

Always put your baby to sleep on his back, not on his tummy.

. . .

Avoid soft comforters and pillows. Instead use a firm crib mattress, and put your baby in a blanket sleeper if it's cool. Babies old enough to roll over can suffocate if they lie facedown on a quilt or soft pillow.

. . .

Should you let your baby sleep with you? It's a controversial topic, with the Consumer Product Safety Commission warning that an average of fifteen babies are suffocated each year while sleeping with their parents. However, babies and their parents have been sleeping together for centuries, and it's a wonderful way to bond with your little one. One solution: make your bed safer for baby by using a Sleep-A-Bye cushion, which can hold your baby safely and securely in one spot. Or purchase a three-sided crib that attaches to the side of your bed, so that a parent can reach and touch baby—and lift him out easily for feedings—but can't roll over on him. These cribs are fairly new, but you can find them in some infant stores or on the Internet. Another option is simply to put your baby to sleep in a bassinet next to your bed.

. . .

If you put your baby to sleep with a pacifier, always roll a small washrag inside the loop of the pacifier. Otherwise, your baby may bruise himself by rolling onto the hard edge of the pacifier.

SPECIAL PLAYS

In the evening, or before bedtime, try these relaxing activities:

Play nature tapes, such as repetitive ocean sounds or rainfall.

• • •

Try vacuuming. No kidding. Many babies find the noise of a vacuum soothing, so pop your baby into his swing, set him in motion, and let him supervise your housecleaning.

• • •

Play with soft, quiet toys such as stuffed animals and rubber toys, rather than squeaky toys or toys that make music or light up.

• • •

Buy a porch swing for your front yard, and spend part of your evenings together watching the world go by.

• • •

While bright lights and music can keep a fussy baby awake, soft lights and music can be soothing.

• • •

Do the laundry together. Babies like snug, warm places like a laundry room, and many of them love the rhythmic, relaxing whump-a-whump sound of the dryer. Plus, you'll earn points with your partner. And it's not like you don't have enough laundry right now.

• • •

Do you have a bassinet on wheels? If so, bring it into the family room, pop your baby in it, and gently roll it back and forth while you're watching TV—or put your baby in his bouncing seat and keep him next to you on the sofa.

ADVICE FROM THE COACH

Our baby sleeps just fine in the car, on the couch, on our laps—everywhere but in bed. Any ideas?

Try renting a special crib insert, called a Rock 'N' Comfort, that moves gently and plays womb music, soothing your baby to sleep. It's available from high-end baby stores, for about $250 for six months. Fisher Price's Slumber Time Soother music box also can comfort a baby who's afraid of being alone in his crib. If these don't help, try letting your swaddled baby fall asleep on your bed, and then moving him to a bassinet in your room afterward. Some gentle pats on the back may help him settle down quickly again.

Here's another tip: make a tape of yourself or your baby's mom humming, singing, or talking to your baby. Purchase a tape recorder that can be set to play the tape continuously.

Our new baby barely sleeps at all, and he's constantly fussing during the day. We're exhausted. What can we do?

Some babies—I call them high-need babies—are particularly hard to calm. The most important thing to know is that this isn't your fault—it's just the way they're born.

In general, high-need babies calm down after the first six months when their digestive systems and nervous systems mature. So keep telling yourself, *this will pass.* In the meantime, avoid overstimulating your baby with too many sights and sounds. Give him simple toys that only stimulate

56

one sense at a time—crib mirrors or stuffed animals, for instance. Put him in his bouncer seat or swing frequently, being sure to prop his head securely; most babies find the rhythmic motion soothing. And keep your home as quiet as possible—no loud TV, rock music, or computer games.

Our baby sleeps only about forty-five minutes to an hour and a half at a time, and he wakes up five or six times a night. I have a high-stress job, and I need my rest. Help!

It takes time for babies to learn to sleep for long periods. How *much* time depends, in part, on the size of your baby, whether or not he was born prematurely, and whether or not he fell into sync with your partner's sleep cycle while he was still in the womb.

If your baby's wake-up calls are so disruptive that they're hurting your performance at work, consider putting his crib in a different room. Or sack out on the living room couch on those nights when sleep is critical. Then, on the weekends, get up with the baby during the night and let your partner rest. By spelling each other, you'll each get a few good nights of sleep per week—which is about all you can realistically expect right now.

My mother keeps criticizing the way my partner cares for our baby—the bathwater is too warm, the bottles aren't warm enough, etc., etc. Mom says she's just trying to help, and it's true that she raised four kids herself, so she's an expert. But my partner says Mom's interference is driving her crazy. I'm stuck in the middle— what do I do to make both of them happy?

You can't. Instead, as tactfully as you can, stand up for your partner. Your relationship with her takes precedence over your relationship with your mother. Besides, while your mom means well, her well-intentioned criticisms are harmful if they're making your partner feel threatened. If your mother can't resist the urge to criticize, tell her to pass her suggestions on to you, in private.

Also, be aware that your mother's ideas may be a little outdated. Many of the things that moms used to do—for instance, giving two-week-old babies cereal, or putting a little whiskey in their bottles to make them sleep—are definitely "out" now. While your mom may be more experienced, your partner's likely to be more up-to-date on what's safe and healthy for your baby.

I think my partner gives in to our baby too much. She picks him up every time he cries, rocks him to sleep instead of simply putting him in his crib, and feeds him every couple of hours—even at night. Is she spoiling him?

Don't worry—it's impossible to spoil a newborn! Toddlers, yes. Teenagers, definitely. But not newborns. Right now your baby needs to eat every few hours, and he needs plenty of cuddling and reassurance, too. The world is still a strange and frightening place to him, and he probably feels much as you would if you were suddenly dropped onto an alien planet. You and Mom are his constants, and he needs to touch and smell you near him. He also misses the gentle motion of moving in the womb, which rocking can simulate. As he ages, he'll sleep longer, eat less frequently, and become more independent.

My partner frequently falls asleep when she lies down with our baby. I wish she wouldn't, because I want some time with her.

Try putting the baby down yourself; for some reason, babies often go down for bedtime better if Dad's in charge. This is an especially good idea if your partner has just returned to work and is exhausted at the end of the day, or if she's been home all day with the baby and needs some R and R.

CHAPTER FOUR

The End Run: Surviving Those Dirty Diapers

Exercises from Birth to Twelve Months

Okay, so it's not a topic you want to discuss. But you'll spend a lot of time thinking about it over the next couple of years. For instance, you'll wonder:

- How can such a little person hold so much poop?
- How can she poop so often?
- Why is it green?
- Why is it yellow?
- Why is it liquid?
- What do I do if she poops at a restaurant? At the boss's house? At the mall?

Some of these questions have no answers. There's no explanation for the fact that a little one-month-old baby can, seemingly, produce poops bigger than your dog. Others, however, are simple. The color of your baby's poop, for instance, is mostly a result of what she eats. Breast-fed babies tend to have pale, inoffensive bowel movements, while babies at the solid food stage have hideous poops in shades of avocado green, harvest gold, and khaki.

The Big Question, of course, is, What do I do with that disgusting diaper? In previous generations, the answer was simple: "Here, let me hand you over to Mommy—she'll fix you right up." But things have changed, and men now change diapers as often as women. And you'll need to get a grip on this skill early on, because it'll be a l-o-o-o-ng time before you toss that last dirty diaper. Your baby will need about ten changes a day at first, and about *six thousand* diapers over the course of the next two to three years.

Don't worry, though, because diapering gets easier as you go along. Like many life events that seem, at first, to be too awful to survive—boot camp, your first job, life with your college roommate—you'll find that it gets more bearable with time. Also, you'll get much faster at it, so the torture won't last as long.

In fact, the smartest way to approach dirty diapers is in the manner that pit crews approach a repair. Have all of your tools at hand, ready to go at a moment's notice, and you'll be done in half the time it takes a less organized dad. Here's what you'll need:

- A changing pad.
- A good supply of diapers. Lay one out in the ready position.
- Cloths for cleaning baby's bottom. Skip the wipes, except for trips. I'll explain why at the end of this chapter.
- Corn starch–based powder, to help your baby stay dry. You can also blow dry your baby with a hair dryer after a change, if there's an outlet handy. Be sure, of course, that the hair dryer is on a low setting!
- Baby lotion or diaper rash ointment, if you use it.
- Plastic diaper covers, if you use cloth diapers without built-in linings.
- Rattles or other washable toys.
- A spare cloth or disposable diaper that you can use as a quick cover-up if you're changing a boy who decides to pee in your face.

Now, here's what you do:

- Place your baby on the changing pad. KEEP ONE HAND ON HER AT ALL TIMES, or fasten the changing pad strap around her, unless you're changing her on the floor. You'd be surprised how many babies fall off changing tables when a parent turns away for just an instant to grab a diaper.
- If you have a few extra seconds, put a wrist rattle on your baby's arm, or place an interesting musical toy where she can watch it. If there's a musical mobile near the changing table, wind it up. If you keep her occupied, she'll wiggle less.

- Rip open the tabs on the old diaper.
- Now, here comes the tricky part. Grasp your baby's feet, lift her butt a few inches off the old diaper, and give her a thorough wipe. Be sure to get all the nooks and crannies, because even a little leftover poop can give your baby a rash. During this process, keep an eye on your baby's feet, because babies have a real knack for sticking their feet in their poop. If you're cleaning a girl, be sure to wipe her from front to back, to protect against urinary tract infections. Once your baby's bottom is really clean, move the old diaper out of the way, and whisk the new diaper under her.
- Apply lotion, diaper rash ointment, or corn starch–based baby powder. If you use powder, shake it gently and be careful not to create a cloud, because you don't want your baby breathing it. If you're using a blow dryer, give your baby a quick dry on low heat. Quickly pull up the front of the diaper and fasten it to the back using the sticky tabs—*very* quickly, if you're diapering a boy, so you don't get squirted. If you're using cloth diapers without built-in covers, put on the plastic diaper cover.
- Finish dressing your baby, put her in a safe place, and then dispose of the diaper fast. Congratulations— you're done!

Things get trickier, of course, if you're not at home when your baby lets loose. That's one reason I told you to keep a changing pad in your car. If you can't find a clean rest room where you can change your baby, the backseat of the car—or even the trunk—will do in a pinch, as long as you have a changing pad or a blanket between your upholstery and all that mess. You'll also want to carry a supply of plastic grocery bags in the diaper bag, so you can tie up really stinky diapers in two or even three bags before discarding them. If you're at a friend's house, take the bagged diaper outside to the trash—otherwise, you'll probably never be invited back.

CLOTH OR DISPOSABLE?

If you're interested in protecting the environment, you'll probably consider using cloth diapers. On the downside, this creates astronomically more work for you and Mom—and all those wet diapers will make your house or apartment smell like an outhouse. On the upside, cloth diapers are now available with Velcro fasteners (no more diaper pins), built-in covers (no more plastic pants), and even gathered waists and legs.

If you manage to stick with cloth diapers, good for you. If you don't, don't feel too guilty—hardly anyone else does, either. Moreover, the cloth versus disposables argument isn't as clear-cut as it seems, because cloth diapers require a lot of washing and drying—and that uses plenty of electricity and water. However, cloth does appear to have the edge environmentally, and you'll save a lot of money if you can stand the extra work and the smell.

PRACTICE MAKES PERFECT

It'll take your newborn baby a few days to get the hang of having bowel movements. After all, this is a new job for her. Her first production will be a strange-looking green-and-black poop called meconium. It looks scary, but it's perfectly natural—just leftovers from your baby's stay in the womb.

Your baby's first poops may scare the daylights out of her, because they're a new experience. After a couple of days, however, she'll be a regular poop machine. Sometimes, however, just like a grown-up, she'll have a little trouble getting things moving. She'll need to poop three to five times a day, and at first it's a challenge to coordinate all of the activities required to have a bowel movement. Occasionally, too, your baby may get a bad case of gas—especially if she's nursing and Mom eats broccoli, cabbage, beans, or other gassy foods.

Unlike you, your baby can't just chug some Gas-X when she's bloated, and she doesn't know what to do when she can't get a poop out. At these times, the simple exercises that follow can ease her discomfort and make life a lot easier for both of you. In addition, these "End Run" activities will help your baby learn skills she'll use later when she rolls, sits up, crawls, and walks.

"Gassed Up"

Birth to Six Months

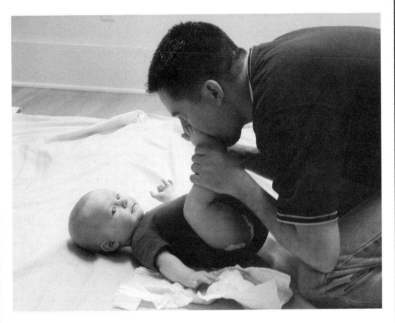

Remember the last time you ordered a chili burger and onion rings for lunch, and then had to suffer through a three-hour business meeting? Then you can sympathize with your gassy baby, because there's nothing more miserable than being full of methane and not being able to let it out. This exercise can help a gassy baby relieve herself and also can help a constipated baby to get things moving.

- With your baby on her back, either on the floor or on your lap, use the flat part of your palm to gently massage her tummy muscles from side to side. Don't use your fingertips. Gently massage for about three minutes.

- Slowly raise your baby's legs, so they're close to her tummy. While supporting her knees, gently roll her from side to side for about three minutes.
- Gently push your baby's feet against your chest. This will give her some stability to push when she's trying to release a poop or some pesky gas.
- Repeat, if your baby is enjoying these exercises.

GAME TIP: *When your baby first starts eating solid food, she may have trouble with constipation. This problem usually resolves itself as your baby's system adjusts to her new food, but if it persists, ask your pediatrician about what can help to loosen her up.*

"Place Kick I"

Six Weeks to Six Months

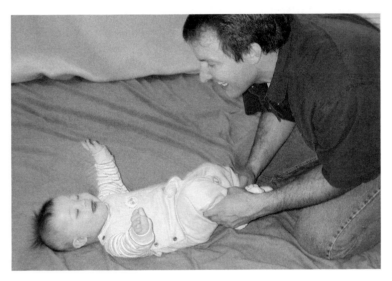

Think your baby could be the next Mia Hamm or Brandi Chastain? Start her out early, by practicing imaginary soccer goals. This exercise will build her crawling and walking skills, and also help strengthen the tummy muscles she uses to poop.

Part 1

- Before or after a diaper change, put a soft towel or blanket under your baby's head—or use a crescent head support for newborns—so her head is well supported and centered.
- Place both of your baby's feet on the changing surface. Push down gently on your baby's knees, to

give her the sensation of supporting weight on her feet.

- Next, lift your baby's left leg, making your movements slow and gentle and keeping her right foot on the changing table or floor. Repeat with opposite legs. Your baby's leg shouldn't go higher than an angle of ninety-degrees to her body.
- To make this exercise more fun for your baby, nibble on her toes, kiss them, or count them.

GAME TIP: *This is an especially good exercise for babies with low muscle tone.*

Part 2

- Place your baby on her back on the floor.
- Holding your baby's legs gently around the ankles, lift them a short distance off the ground, then lift them a bit higher, and then lift them higher still. Say "Up-up-up!" at each stage. Be sure to make your movements gentle.
- Bring your baby's legs back down in three steps, saying "Down-down-down!"
- Do the same exercise with your baby's arms, supporting her at the shoulders. Begin with her arms by her sides, and raise them in three steps, saying, "Up-up-up!" Then lower them in three stages, saying, "Down-down-down!"

GAME TIP: *Be sure to pause for one to two seconds at each stage as you raise your baby's arms or legs. This helps teach her to make graded rather than all-or-nothing muscle movements.*

"Tug-of-War"

Six to Twelve Months

Take advantage of diaper time by teaching new skills. This exercise helps build your baby's shoulder and arm stability, which is important for everything from tennis to basketball. In addition, it'll help her learn to reach forward, and it will improve her eye-hand coordination—a critical skill if she decides to become a Wimbledon contender!

- While your baby is still on the changing table or the floor after a diaper change, lean over her with an old sock or a diaper in your mouth.

- Encourage your baby to reach up to grab the sock. Growl playfully and pretend that you're keeping it away from her. After a little while, let her "win" by successfully pulling the sock from your mouth.

GAME TIP: *If your baby is just learning to reach forward, provide stability during this activity by cupping and supporting her shoulders.*

"Bicycle"

Six to Twelve Months

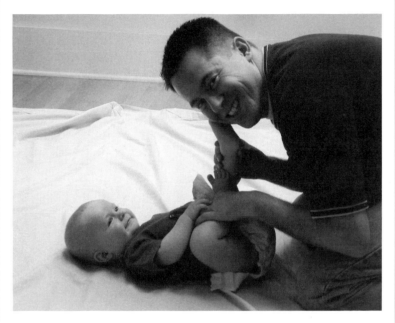

This is another good poop promoter.

- Place your baby tummy-up on the floor.
- Bend your baby's legs at the hips and knees, and encourage her to push her feet against your hands and move her legs in a bicycling motion.
- Move her legs from side to side, keeping them bent.
- Sing to your baby:

> "We're going on a bear hunt
> I'm not afraid

Can't get over it
Can't get under it
We'll bike right through!"

• If your baby is at least six months old, try the motorboat variation of this exercise. Gently grasp each of your baby's legs below the knee and move them alternately in a bicycle motion. Gradually increase the speed. Sing the "Motorboat Song" in time to your baby's cycling, slowing down during the slow line and speeding up during the next two:

"Motorboat, motorboat, go so slow.
Motorboat, motorboat, go so fast.
Motorboat, motorboat, step on the gas!"

"Team Sing-a-Long"
Three to nine Months

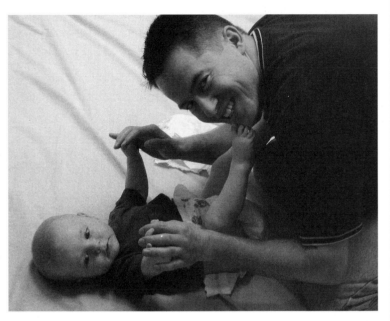

Believe it or not, diaper time can be quality time. Use this opportunity to sing some old favorites to your little one.

- After diapering your baby, hold her hands and sing your favorite baby songs to her.

  Some favorites are:

            "Let's go riding on an elevator.
            First Floor.
            Second Floor.

Third Floor.
Down!"

Lift your baby's arms in stages for each line, and then lower them at the end.

> "I'm bringing home a baby bumblebee,
> Won't my daddy be so proud of me,
> Bringing home a baby bumblebee,
> ZZZZZ he got me!"

Add a daddy tickle with the last line.

- Ask, "How big are you?" Then lift your baby's arms and say, "So big!"
- Say "Touchdown!" and lift your baby's arms. Cheer and say, "Go, Hannah, go!"

"Tummy Games"

Two to Six Months

By encouraging your baby to raise her legs, this activity puts the squeeze on her intestines and will help push a bowel movement through.

- Lay your baby on the sofa, or on a soft blanket on the floor.
- Put your mouth to your baby's tummy, and give her a big kiss or blow a raspberry. Repeat several times. When you do this, your baby's legs will lift in response.

GAME TIP: *This exercise also helps build strong tummy muscles.*

TIPS FOR WINNING

If you're handy at carpentry, put some easy-to-reach shelves above your baby's changing table. You'll be able to reach the baby powder, lotion, etc., and your baby won't.

• • •

Does your baby get severe diaper rash? Experiment with different brands of diapers. Some babies who break out when wearing one brand do fine in another. Also, change wet diapers frequently so they aren't in contact with your baby's skin for long. Drying your baby's bottom with a hair dryer set on low may help reduce bacteria-caused rashes, too.

• • •

Give your baby's bottom a good cleaning, even if she's merely wet and not dirty. You'll help protect her against diaper rash.

• • •

If your baby wets her diaper *and* her clothes, avoid taking the easy way out and changing just the diaper. The job isn't done until the wet clothes come off, too.

• • •

Admit it: Are you tempted, when your baby poops on your watch, to leave her dirty diaper on, and then say, "She just went!" when your partner arrives back home? If so, resist the urge. Your baby's sensitive skin can develop a rash after a short time in contact with a dirty diaper. And besides, your partner won't believe you.

• • •

If you have a dog, you may discover that he thinks baby poop is a gourmet treat. If so, buy yourself a Diaper Genie or similar disposable diaper pail that your dog can't access. Diaper Genies and similar products also keep your home virtually free of diaper odors and make diaper disposal much easier and more sanitary.

THE SAFETY ZONE

Never leave your baby unattended on a changing table or counter, even for an instant. Babies roll when you least expect it.

• • •

Always wash your hands after a diaper change.

• • •

When you need to move your baby while dressing or changing her, support her head and roll her to her side rather than pulling her up by her arms. If she is under one year of age, you could dislocate her shoulder by pulling her up by her arms.

• • •

If you use warmed wipes, or clean your baby's bottom with heated water, check the temperature before touching your baby's skin.

SPECIAL PLAYS

To make diaper time more fun, make faces at your baby— or make funny sounds. If you're entertaining enough, your baby will hold still longer. Better yet, invent a special diaper changing song.

Encourage your baby to lift her legs—a good way to relieve gas and get a poop under way—by dressing her feet in patterned or striped socks, or socks with bells or faces. Your baby will enjoy watching and reaching for these moving targets.

ADVICE FROM THE COACH

I feel like a wuss. I guess I'm overly squeamish, but the smell of a dirty diaper makes me want to throw up. Everyone laughs at me except my partner, who's mad at me because I won't handle diaper changes.

If you're like most dads, you'll find that you get used to the smell in time. However, some people do have an exceptionally sensitive sense of smell, and you may be one of them. If dirty diapers continue to turn your stomach, try rubbing Vicks VapoRub under your nose before you change your baby's diaper. Some guys say it helps a lot. You can also try using those disposable masks sold at paint stores.

Our pediatrician told us to use cloths instead of baby wipes when we change our baby. It's such a nuisance—is there a good reason for this?

Yes. Believe it or not, many baby wipes contain both alcohol and irritating chemicals. You wouldn't want to rub them on your own skin, much less your baby's! A cloth dipped in warm water is much easier on your baby's bottom and won't lead to a flaming diaper rash that will make your baby—and you—miserable. Reserve commercial wipes for occasional use when you're away from home.

I'm concerned about the environment, and I think we should use cloth diapers. My partner says they're too much work. You wouldn't believe how much we've argued about this.

This one is easy. If you feel strongly about the cloth versus disposable issue, offer to handle the extra work involved in using cloth diapers yourself—putting the diapers out for the diaper service, folding them, and putting them away. And be reasonable about using disposable diapers when you're traveling, or visiting friends.

My baby won't lie still on the changing table while I diaper her. I get so frustrated when she wiggles and the diaper gets all twisted up.

Life would certainly be more convenient if babies stayed in one spot during diaper changes! But infants are naturally on the move, because that's how they learn about their world. Also, diapering is stressful for some babies at first, and they instinctively respond by pulling up or away. This is a temporary problem, since babies quickly get *lots* of practice when it comes to having their diapers changed.

It's best to change a squirmy baby on the floor, so you don't have to worry about falls. To help distract her, give your baby a rattle or toy. And don't clutch her too tightly; some dads accidentally bruise their babies, because they're hanging on so desperately to a leg or an arm.

I'm a computer technician, and I can fix hardware problems with one hand tied behind my back—but give me a baby and a diaper, and everything goes wrong. Am I just an idiot when it comes to parenting?

No, you're a rookie. When you first learned to play basketball, did your coach stick you in the middle of a game with a bunch of experienced guys and expect you to play like a pro? No—he taught you how to shoot hoops, and how to dribble and guard and pass, and eventually you put all the pieces together and learned to play basketball.

Similarly, you'll probably find that it's easiest to learn diapering in stages. Start out with a dry baby—or even a doll—and a dry diaper, and literally do a dry run. Then start changing a couple of wet diapers every day. Once you've learned to get the diapers on straight, and just snug enough so they won't leak, you're ready for the bombs. By the way, if you have perpetual problems with diaper leaks, try a different brand; some fit far more snugly than others. Or, when you are buying diapers, try a larger size.

My partner stands over me and criticizes me when I diaper the baby. It makes me nervous, and I screw up.

Make an agreement that she'll leave the room when you change a diaper. Also, remind her that because women have usually spent more time baby-sitting infants, or playing at diapering dolls, they generally have more practice at changing diapers than men. Tell her to be patient and give you a little time to perfect your skills.

CHAPTER FIVE

The Handoff: When Mom Leaves You Alone with the Baby

Exercises for Six Weeks and Upward

Is there anything more terrifying than being left in charge of a tiny, helpless infant who's totally dependent on you?

Yes—when that baby opens his mouth and starts to scream.

Sooner or later, however, it's going to happen to you. After all, tempting as the idea sounds, you can't *really* expect your partner to stay home day and night for three solid years. One day she's casually going to say, "I'm off to the store—you watch the baby."

When she does, stay calm. If you mastered the diaper change rules in the last chapter, you're already prepared for the worst part of baby tending. The rest is easy, if you know a few simple tricks.

PLAN AHEAD

With any job, you're better off being prepared and having all of the necessary tools at hand—and this job is no exception. Before your partner leaves home, make sure you have everything you'll need for baby tending. That includes a ready-to-go changing area (see previous chapter) stocked with twice as many diapers as you think you'll need; several changes of clothes, some spare blankets, and a supply of burp rags; favorite toys, music, and videos; a list of emergency phone numbers; prepared formula or breast milk in the fridge, as well as food and a baby spoon, if your baby is old enough for solid food; and a car seat, just in case you need to drive your baby somewhere.

Also, if you're feeling insecure, ask your partner to take a cell phone, if she has one. That way, you can give her a call if you're in over your head. Just don't be surprised if she laughs and hangs up.

WHAT THE HECK DOES HE *WANT*?

The next trick is to learn how to decode your baby's cries. This is a valuable skill, because 98 percent of the work of baby-tending involves figuring out how to stop them from hollering. Most babies start with a low-grade cry and work their way up to spectacular wails, so you'll want to intervene early on to forestall a crisis.

Babies have four standard cries, and often you can tell which is which by looking for the following clues:

1. The "I'm lonely/bored, pick me up!" cry is a mildly uncomfortable, annoyed, low-pitched sound.
2. The "I'm tired/fussy" or the "I'm wet/uncomfortable" cry is a low, intermittent whine that starts with occasional fussing and then increases in intensity.
3. The "I'm hungry—feed me!" cry is often accompanied by your baby rubbing his cheek against you. This cry tends to stop and start like an engine ignition that's not getting enough fuel, and it's usually accompanied by sucking noises.
4. The "My tummy hurts/I'm trying to poop" cry is generally intense and urgent, and your baby will probably pull his legs up.

No matter what type of cry you hear, your first action should be to pick your baby up—and fast, because the longer he cries, the harder it'll be for him to stop. Hold him close for a few minutes, soothing him with some calm words, and walk him around the house. This will give you a little breathing room while you analyze what he's after.

While you're calming your baby, check to see if his diaper is wet, and if it is, change it (see diapering tips in Chapter 4). If not, listen to his communication. If you detect a tired/fussy cry, pop your baby into his swing or simply snuggle with him for a little while, and then put him down for a nap. If that doesn't work, take him for a walk in his stroller, either outdoors or around the house, or take him for a ride in the car. (See Chapter 3 for other suggestions.)

If you think you're hearing a poop cry, or if your baby is grunting or squirming, place him on a blanket on the floor and gently massage his tummy. Once he succeeds in going, change him fast, so his skin doesn't get irritated; otherwise, you'll be in for another bout of crying later.

A low-grade, chronic fussing, on the other hand, may mean that your baby is bored, or missing Mom. If so, he's in need of a daddy snuggle and a story to distract him. Also, see the exercises and activities in this chapter, which are designed to please a baby who's looking for some entertainment.

Of course, if it's the feed me! cry, the solution is obvious: it's mealtime. For many men, this is a scary thought. If your partner breast-feeds, you might not have much practice at giving a baby a bottle—and even if you use formula, you're probably used to getting the easy feeding times, when your baby is happy and sleepy and your better half is there to take over at the first sign of hysteria—yours or your baby's. This time you're on your own, but with a few simple preparations, you'll do fine.

First, let's look at the art of getting a bottle of milk or formula down a baby. Then, for when baby grows older, we'll tackle something even more challenging: solid food.

BOTTLES AND BURPS

If your baby is still too young for people food, feeding times are pretty simple. If you have a bottle, a burp rag, a comfortable chair, and a sweatshirt or soft shirt to wear so your baby can cuddle up with you, you're ready to go.

Before giving your baby his bottle, make sure it's the right temperature by testing a few drops on the inside of your wrist. It should feel lukewarm, not hot or cold. If it's too cool, put it in a bowl of hot water. Many experts don't recommend zapping bottles in the microwave, because the formula can heat unevenly. If it's too hot, run it under cold water for a few minutes, or add cold breast milk or formula.

Next, be sure the nipple is on tight. Turn the bottle upside down and squeeze it gently, to ensure that milk will come out. If the nipple is plugged, open the hole with a large clean pin or ice pick. Now, toss your burp rag over your shoulder and find a comfortable spot—preferably a rocking chair—where you can cradle your baby. Be sure he's sitting up almost vertically, so he can swallow better. *Voilà!* You're set.

The important thing at this point, is: *don't rush.* Your baby is used to the feel and smell and sound of Mom, so give him a few minutes to get used to the idea that Dad's in charge now. Cuddle your baby closely, rock him, talk to him softly, soften him up. It's a little like taking your partner out for a nice dinner at a romantic restaurant: you don't just say, "Pack in that fettucine, hon, or we won't get home in time for *Star Trek*." It's the same with your baby: you may be in a hurry to get back to your book or computer game, but he isn't in any hurry at all—and you're on *his* schedule now.

The first step, of course, is to get the nipple into your baby's mouth. Your baby is born with a rooting reflex, which means that if you touch his cheek, he'll turn his head to that side and search for a nipple. You can use this reflex to direct him to his bottle. If he spits it out, gently direct him back to it. Breast-fed babies in particular may need time to accept a bottle, because the texture of a rubber nipple seems peculiar to them.

Once your baby starts sucking, give him time to eat; some babies eat like linebackers, but most like to nurse a little, rest for a bit, and then start again. Be sure you let him eat his fill, because a full baby is a happy baby. If your baby coughs or chokes, however, stop feeding him and bring him immediately into an upright position, and rub his back.

When your baby is truly done, he'll let you know by repeatedly spitting out the nipple, turning his head away, or arching his back. At this point, pop him over your shoulder—*after* positioning your burp rag strategically—and give him quick, gentle pats on the back until he burps. Or, if it's easier, lay him over your lap, tummy

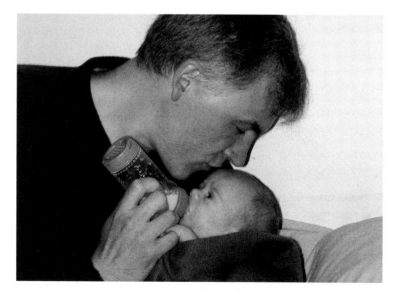

down, and pat or rub his back. Remember to move the burp rag to cover your pants. Some babies don't burp much, while others are lusty belchers. If your baby tends to be gassy, or feeds for a long time, you'll want to throw in a few extra burps in midfeeding. Don't be surprised if he spits up on you; it's normal. And be sure to burp him even if he's fallen asleep—otherwise, he's likely to wake up later with gas and make your life miserable.

One caution: don't give your baby more than one bottle at a single feeding, even if he seems to want more. Babies have a limited capacity, and if you offer that second bottle, its contents are likely to wind up all over the front of your shirt.

FEEDING THE OLDER BABY

If your baby is old enough for solid foods, mealtime is more complicated—and way, way messier. You'll definitely want to change into old clothes for this event.

The first step, once you're properly attired, is to get organized. Dish out small amounts from each jar of baby food, putting the jars back in the fridge after they're opened. don't feed your baby directly from the jars—or, if you do, toss out the jars afterward. Otherwise, germs can grow in the unused food. You can warm up cereals, meats, and vegetables in the microwave; just be sure to stir them afterward, and test them to make sure they're not too hot. Put the food, a small spoon, a bib, a clean-up rag, and your baby's cup, with a small amount of juice or milk in it, where you can reach them.

Next, put your baby in his high chair or infant seat. Be sure the seat is in a safe place, and don't leave your baby unattended. Snap the bib around his neck.

Scoop a small bit of food onto the spoon, put the spoon in your baby's mouth, and wait for him to use his upper lip to take the food off the spoon. Be patient with him, because he may spit out a few bites while he's getting used to the taste. If he keeps spitting out his food, or starts crying, check to see if he's thirsty. If not, he's probably not hungry; take a break and try again later. Otherwise, keep feeding him until he loses interest and turns his face away. Two to three teaspoons of each food is plenty for a baby just beginning to eat solids, while an older infant may eat a quarter cup or even more at a sitting. Give your baby occasional sips of his milk, and when he's all done, clean his face and hands with a wet cloth or paper towel.

A few words of warning: it's best to stick with foods your baby already likes, rather than introducing new foods on your watch. Also, even if you're feeding your baby his very favorite goodies, wear an old T-shirt and keep your distance, because no food is truly safe—and one thing you'll learn early on is that creamed spinach and pureed carrots really stain.

"ENTERTAIN ME!"

If your baby's crying even though he isn't hungry, tired, wet, or working on a poop, his fussing probably means, "I'm lonely! Pick me up!" This is the easiest of all baby problems to fix. The simplest solution is to pick your baby up and give him a tour of the house, showing off all of your stuff—"Look! An oven mitt!" "Wow—it's a clock radio!" Remember, he rarely gets a close-up look at your paintings, magazines, and kitchen gadgets, so your mundane junk is fascinating to him. Show him how the window shades go up and down, and how the doors open and shut. Let him touch knobs and feel textures and surfaces, listen to the clock ticking, and hear the water running in the sink. Play with closing and opening the drapes or blinds, so your baby can enjoy the contrast between light and dark.

Or, if you've both been inside all day, go outside and investigate the yard. Show him the trees, the birdhouse, the mailbox. Turn on the hose and let him see the water come out. If you have wind chimes, let him touch them. Put a blanket on the grass, and give him a worm's-eye view of the grass and the bugs, making sure he doesn't eat them. Everything in the great outdoors is new and exciting to your baby, especially with Dad along as a tour guide.

Also, give your baby a workout by doing the following activities with him. They're designed to keep a playful baby amused and entertained, as well as to help develop motor coordination and language and thinking skills. Another plus: they'll help your baby work off excess energy, so he's likely to take a long nap afterward.

One last word on the subject of cries: if your baby doesn't seem to need a nap, a poop, a dry diaper, entertainment, a cuddle, or food, look for less obvious causes. Make sure that he isn't too warm or too cold, and that he's not feverish. And if he's the sensitive type, turn off the TV and shut the windows to block out noise; he may just be overstimulated and need a little peace and quiet.

NOTE: *Check the age ranges at the top of each exercise, and select the ones that are right for your baby.*

"Touchdown"

Two to Five Months

This game is a big hit with babies and promotes shoulder stability.

- Put your baby on his back, either on the sofa or on the floor. Use a blanket if you're doing this on the floor.
- Gently grasp each of your baby's arms and lift them gently.
- As you lift your baby's arms over his head say, "Touchdown!" After you've practiced this, lift your own arms, say "Touchdown!" and encourage your baby to lift his arms in imitation.

GAME TIP: *Make your movements slow and gradual.*

"Backfield in Motion"

Three to Eight Months

An exercise that will simultaneously teach your baby balance, help him learn to shift his weight in response to motion, and work on your love handles.

- Lie on your back on the floor, with a pillow under your head. Bend your legs and place your baby on your legs, lying between your feet and your knees and facing toward you on his tummy. Be sure his arms are forward, as shown.
- Slowly rock your legs from side to side, and forward and back. Be sure to support your baby very carefully so he doesn't fall.

GAME TIP: *Be very careful not to raise your feet too high during this exercise—you don't want your baby to do a nosedive! Also, always do this exercise on a padded surface.*

93

"Weightlifter"

Two to Six Months

Here's another exercise that benefits both you and your baby. You'll be helping your infant learn to develop his back muscles in preparation for sitting while you're giving your biceps a workout at the same time.

- Stand, holding your baby under his arms with your hands. Slowly lift his face to yours and give him a kiss.
- Gradually lower your baby back to chest level, and repeat.

GAME TIP: *Avoid tossing your baby while doing this exercise. Your hands should be holding him at all times.*

"Stunt Pilot"

Six Weeks to Four Months

As your baby watches your plane, he'll be learning to follow an object with his eyes. He'll also learn to reach forward as he tries to touch the plane, and he'll be honing his eye-hand coordination.

- While cradling your baby in one arm, fly a paper airplane near him with your other hand.
- Touch the plane to different parts of his body, saying, "Got your tummy!" "Got your legs!" "Got your fingers!"
- If your baby is very young, move the plane slowly. As his eye-tracking skills improve, move the plane faster, and switch between horizontal and vertical flights.

GAME TIP: *When you play this game, touch each body part several times, saying its name each time. Also, repeatedly say "Stop!" and "Go!" as you move the plane. The repetition will help your baby understand new vocabulary words.*

"Sports Page I"

Two to nine Months

He's way too young to care who won the Stanley Cup or the Kentucky Derby, but your baby will enjoy snuggling with you as you read the paper together. He'll also be hearing some new words, and learning to sit still in preparation for long dad-and-child afternoons at the ballpark years from now.

- Sit on the couch or in a cozy chair with your baby, and read the newspaper together. Read some of the words out loud, so your baby can enjoy the sound of your voice. Also, point to photos—"See the basketball!" "That's a car!"

GAME TIP: *Your baby will also enjoy grabbing for and wrinkling the paper.*

"Peekaboo Play-Offs"

Three-and-a-Half to Eight Months

This old favorite helps your baby learn object permanence—the concept that an object (or Mom or Dad) still exists, even if he can't see it. It also helps your baby learn to reach forward and to imitate, and it builds shoulder stability and arm strength.

- Cover your face with your hands.
- Say "Peekaboo!," uncover your face, and give your baby a big smile.
- Repeat, covering your baby's face instead of yours. Use a small baby washcloth.

GAME TIP: *You can also play this game by hiding your hand or foot, your baby's hand or foot, or a toy partially under a washrag, and saying, "Peekaboo!" as you uncover it.*

"Floor Routine"

Six Weeks to Twenty-Four Months

For babies, dancing can be a learning experience. As you waltz across your living room floor, you'll be improving your baby's balance, head control, listening skills, and appreciation of rhythm. You'll also be helping him learn to reach forward with his arms.

- Holding your baby firmly, dance around your living room with him. If your baby is young, be sure to support his head carefully.
- Be careful not to bounce or toss your baby while dancing with him.

GAME TIP: *Try dancing to different rhythms and styles of music: fast, slow, jazz, classical, rock, etc. This helps your baby begin to learn concepts such as fast/slow and loud/soft.*

"Air Races"

Three to Nine Months

Kids love the feeling of flying, and babies are no exception. Your infant will enjoy moving through the air in Dad's strong grasp, and he'll be improving his head, neck, and back alignment and learning to lift his body against gravity.

- Holding your baby securely under his arms, lift him to your shoulder level and fly him around the room. Be careful to move fairly slowly, so you don't frighten him.
- Each time your baby comes in for a landing near your face, give him a big kiss.

GAME TIP: *When you're doing exercises that involve lifting your baby, be sure he's dressed in clothes that aren't too loose or bulky. Otherwise, you may have difficulty holding him firmly.*

"Baby NASCAR"

Three Months to One Year

Your baby's always a backseat passenger in the car, but in this exercise he'll have a chance to be in the driver's seat. His driving lesson will familiarize him with new words, develop coordination, and give him a chance to cuddle with Dad, all at the same time.

- Hold your baby in your lap. Enjoy playing together with a toy steering wheel. Say "beep beep!" "zoom," and "rmmmmm," and make other car noises.
- Talk about where you're driving: "Going to the store!" "Off to the ocean!"

GAME TIP: *This is fun to play in front of a mirror.*

"Sock-er"

Six to Twelve Months

Memory games are fun and improve your baby's thinking skills. For this one, you'll need some colorful old socks and small cardboard tubes. A toilet paper roll is perfect.

- Put your baby in his infant seat, or if he's old enough, have him sit on the floor.
- While your baby is watching, insert the sock partway into the tube. Say, "Where's the sock? Look around!" When your baby focuses on the sock and tube, point to it and say, "It's in here!" Help your baby grasp the sock and pull it out.

- Next, give your baby a tube and a sock, and take a tube and a sock yourself. Show your baby how you hide your sock in your tube, and then help him hide his sock in his tube.

GAME TIP: *This game helps teach the concept of object permanence—the knowledge that an object still exists, even when it can't be seen.*

"Switch Play"

Eight to Twenty-four Months

This simple activity gives your baby an important lesson in cause and effect. He'll also learn the concept of on/off, practice refined finger movements in preparation for writing, coloring, buttoning, and zipping, and use his imitation skills as he follows your lead.

- Show your baby how to flip the light switch on.
- Show your baby what happens when he flips the light switch off.

GAME TIP: *If you have different types of lights—for instance, lights with dimmer knobs, or clapper lights—show your baby how these work, too. He won't be able to operate these himself, but he'll enjoy watching Dad do it.*

TIPS FOR WINNING

If your baby is fussy, cradle him against your left side. We don't know why this helps, but one theory is that your baby hears your heartbeat better when he's cuddled on your left. Anyway, even chimps and gorillas follow this rule, so there must be something to it.

•   •   •

It's smart to get in a few practice sessions before your partner leaves you alone with a hungry baby. Take over the bottle-feedings at least two or three nights a week, or try your hand at serving a few dinners if your baby's old enough to eat solid foods.

•   •   •

When you're in charge, be sure you know where to find the telephone number for your baby's pediatrician, in case of an emergency. And remember that pediatricians are understanding people who know how nervous new dads can be—so don't hesitate to call the doctor if you're worried.

•   •   •

Sometimes you can comfort a fussy baby simply by turning on a fan nearby. The white noise is calming, probably because it drowns out background sounds.

•   •   •

Another good way to calm a fussy baby is to let him snuggle against your bare chest. It'll give him a warm, fuzzy feeling—literally!

•   •   •

Baby formula stain on your favorite cotton shirt? Rinse the spot in cold water, soak your shirt in water mixed with a half scoop of enzyme-based laundry detergent, and then wash the shirt in warm or hot water. If there's still a stain, a rust remover designed for fabrics may take it out. As for neckties, blot up water-based stains such as urine, and have other stains cleaned professionally; those toss-in-the-dryer cleaners will get out some but not all baby stains.

• • •

If you're picking out clothes for your baby, choose a shirt that fastens with snaps, because babies tend to dislike having shirts pulled on over their heads. Also, roomy clothes are better than tight outfits. Like you when you're forced to wear a tight necktie or a shirt too small for your waistline, your baby will be uncomfortable if he's stuffed into size-too-small clothes.

THE SAFETY ZONE

Check on your napping baby every half hour to hour.

• • •

If you haven't taken a CPR class and a first aid class, now's the time. Call your local Red Cross or hospital for information.

• • •

Until your child is over three years old, never let him have a toy small enough to fit through a toilet paper tube. He could swallow a toy that small and choke.

• • •

If your baby starts choking, immediately hold him upright, open his mouth, and check for and remove any foreign objects. If he's swallowed a bit of milk the wrong way, hold him upright and pat him on the back until he recovers.

• • •

Each time you put your baby in his high chair, double-check to make sure his tray table is firmly locked in place. Also, be sure to fasten his seat belt.

• • •

When you're horsing around with your baby, watch out for carpet burns. Babies have delicate skin and can develop bad rashes if their skin is rubbed against a carpeted area too quickly.

• • •

It's cute when your dog licks your baby's face, but don't let him do it. Animals can carry and spread salmonella, worms, and other nasty stuff.

• • •

Never toss your baby in the air. It looks like fun, but it could harm his brain or neck.

• • •

Looking for some simple chores you can do while you're housebound with your baby? Here's one: adjust your water heater to a maximum temperature of 110 to 115 degrees. That's where it should stay set for the next few years, to protect your baby from accidental scalding.

SPECIAL PLAYS

Hold your baby in front of a mirror so you can make faces together. From four months onward, put some suction-cup toys on the mirror for him to touch.

•   •   •

When you're home alone with your baby, get out the camera. With the house quiet and no one else around, he's less likely to be distractible, and you may get some great candid shots. The best time to try is right after a meal or a big poop, when he's relaxed and happy. Use a squeaky toy or musical toy to coax a smile, or get his attention by crinkling some paper. Is he sensitive to the flash? If so, take outdoor shots using natural lighting.

•   •   •

Hold your baby on your lap while you surf the Net. He'll enjoy watching the screen and listening to sites that play music. If he's prone to spitting up, however, keep him a safe distance from your keyboard.

•   •   •

Put your baby in a carrier on your chest, and do your housework or yard work. You'll get caught up on chores, and he'll have a ball supervising you.

•   •   •

Here's a simple game that fascinates most babies. Place a toy under a cup, uncover it, and say, "Hurray!" When your baby is around six months or older, move the cup while saying, "Zoom!" and then uncover the toy at the end of the game. By the time he's nine months old, he will be able to uncover the toy himself.

•   •   •

"This Little Piggy" and "The Itsy-Bitsy Spider" are always winners, and both will actually help your baby learn more about his body. If you've forgotten the words to these classic finger games, ask your partner for help, or make some up. Babies aren't too picky.

ADVICE FROM THE COACH

I think my baby hates me. When my partner leaves, he cries non-stop, and nothing I do seems to help. This really upsets me. What am I doing wrong?

Nothing! It's natural for your baby to miss Mom, because she's the person who spends the most time caring for him. Your baby doesn't hate you—he just doesn't *know* you. Babies, much like dogs or cats, learn to recognize people by smell, as well as touch, sound, and sight, and your baby needs to become familiar with your signature scent—something that takes time and lots of close contact.

Also, your baby can pick up on your fear or discomfort. Hold him with confidence, talk to him calmly, wear soft T-shirts or sweats that he can cuddle up to, and—again—just keep emitting those aromas. Unlike everyone else in your family, your baby will grow to love them.

When our baby was a newborn, he'd grab toys and hang on to them tightly. Now that he's about eight weeks old, he drops his toys all the time. Is there something wrong with him?

Relax! He's doing exactly what he should be doing right now. In fact, he's just achieved a major goal. A newborn has an involuntary grasp reflex and can't let go of his toys; your baby's learning to inhibit this reflex, so that he can release and drop toys at will. Although he doesn't grasp toys involuntarily now, he'll develop a voluntary grasp reflex shortly—and that's a much higher-level skill.

Our baby is colicky, and all he does is fuss and cry. I'm supposed to be bonding with him, and instead I can't wait to get out of the house and escape from his shrieking.

It's hell living with a colicky baby, and it's no fun coming home to find your partner crying in the bathroom because she's stressed to the limit by hours of caring for an inconsolable infant. The good news is that your baby will probably outgrow his fussiness in a few months. In the meantime, be a hero and offer to watch him at least once or twice a day so your partner can take a break. Remember, too, that babies can pick up on your own anger or stress and respond with upset tummies.

Colicky babies often respond to motion, so take your baby for a ride in the car or carry him around in a front pack. Also, try laying him over your lap on his tummy, and massaging his back. Another trick is to warm a damp towel in the microwave and place it on your baby's tummy. And for some reason the noise of a vacuum cleaner calms some colicky babies—maybe because it distracts them from their troubles.

What causes colic? We don't know. It's been blamed on abdominal pain, but medications to soothe tummy aches don't seem to help. Sometimes changing formulas solves the problem, but often it doesn't. In fact, the only sure cure for colic is time—so hang in there. Since colic sometimes seems to run in families, you may get your revenge when you're a grandfather.

What's wrong with simply letting my baby cry it out when he's fussy? When I'm in charge, I spend a few minutes trying to calm our baby, but if he's still fussy, I simply put him in his

*crib and shut the door. My partner says this is cruel. Who's
right?*

Crying is a baby's way of communicating "I need some-thing!" To understand how your baby feels when you ignore his cries, imagine how you'd feel if your partner ignored you when you said, "I need a hand with this ladder," or, "I've got a lousy headache and I can't find the asprin."

While your baby's cries can be annoying, remember that he doesn't have the option of sending you a memo or an E-mail, or even hollering out, "Hey! I have a problem here, and I'd appreciate some help, if you don't mind!" All he can do is cry and hope that you'll take his SOS seriously.

*My partner is leaving on a short business trip, and I'll be in charge
for two days. Do I really need to give my baby a bath during that
time? I think I'd rather* smell *a ripe baby than bathe one.*

Your baby can go for two days without a bath and not mind a bit, but bath time is easier than you think. Simply round up the baby shampoo and soap and a towel, and fill the infant tub with a little lukewarm water. If your baby is older, you probably have a bath seat with suction cups that sits in the regular tub. Pop your baby in and give him a gentle wash, starting with the cleaner parts and ending up with his bottom. Be sure to keep a firm grip on him at all times, holding him securely around the back and under the armpit. If you're nervous about dropping him, put the infant tub on the bathroom floor on a large towel, so you won't have far to lift him when it's time to take him out. Wrap him in a towel right away, so he won't get chilled, and then get a diaper on him fast, so he won't undo all of your hard work by peeing on himself.

Better yet, if you're willing to take the risk of being peed on yourself, take a bath in the big tub with your baby on your chest. He'll be safe and secure, and you'll have a nice cuddle together.

The most important rule to remember when bathing your baby is: never, ever leave him alone. Whether he's in a bath seat, a sink, or the big tub, he needs constant supervision.

CHAPTER SIX

Road Games: How to Take Your Baby Out on the Town, Without Losing Your Mind

Exercises from Birth Upward

It used to be so easy. If you wanted to go shopping or visiting, you just got in the car and went. Now it's like staging halftime at the Super Bowl: it takes strategic planning, an astounding amount of special equipment, and nerves of steel. But with the right preparation, you can survive and often even enjoy an outing with your baby.

It's crucial, however, to put yourself in the right frame of mind before you leave the house. If you're a perfectionist who plans every trip down to the last detail and expects everything to go like clockwork ("We'll hit the Virgin Megastore at 11:45, so we can make it to Chili's for lunch by 12:05 . . ."), get over it. Only about 2 percent of the trips you take with your child, for the next sixteen years, will go exactly as you planned. So *expect* things to go awry; then you won't be angry when they do.

BEFORE YOU GO ANYWHERE . . .

The most important piece of equipment you need when you travel with baby—and one that is a legal requirement in every state—is a good infant car seat. Never, never take a trip without one. Also, make sure your car seat is installed correctly; four out of every five car seats aren't. It's one of the most important dad jobs you can do.

Here's how to make sure your baby's seat is safe:

1. Use a rear-facing seat that's the right size for your baby. Newborn babies will require a head support or seat insert, and Velcro seat strap covers.
2. Place the infant seat in the backseat of your car. Babies shouldn't ride in the front seat until they're at least a year old. (If you *must* put your baby in the front seat, be sure the airbag is turned off.)
3. Be sure the seat is firmly secured and doesn't wiggle excessively.
4. Because seat belts with sliding latch plates don't always stay fastened in a crash, buy a locking clip from your car dealer.
5. Be sure to follow the manufacturer's instructions for installing your infant seat. If you have any questions, call the manufacturer.
6. Check to make sure the harness straps fit snugly over your baby's shoulders and lie flat against her chest. The harness clip should be at her armpit level. If your baby slouches in the seat, adjust the angle of the seat.
7. Ask your car dealer to double-check your installation.

Once your car seat passes your safety inspection, you're set to go—almost. All you need are a few dozen essential supplies to keep your baby safe, well fed, well dressed, and entertained while you're away from home.

THE "DON'T LEAVE HOME WITHOUT IT" KIT

If you're like most guys, you will leave it up to your

partner to pack the diaper bag. However, one of these days you'll wind up taking your baby out by yourself—and when you do, a good survival kit is a must. Here's what you'll need:

- A pacifier, a spare pacifier, a pacifier holder, and a spare pacifier for the glove compartment.
- Diapers, diaper rash ointment if needed, and wipes. This is one case in which sensitive-skin commercial baby wipes are handy.
- Bottles of formula and water, with caps.
- Burp cloths.
- Antiseptic hand wipes, in case you need to wash your baby's hands—or for you, in case you get spit up on, pooped on, or peed on.
- *Lots* of plastic bags and paper towels.
- A change of clothes, a sweater or jacket if it's cold, and a hat if you'll be outdoors.
- Sunscreen, if you'll be outdoors.
- A changing pad or blanket.
- If your baby is old enough for solid foods, some Baggies full of dry Cheerios.

Toys, too, are a must. Attach some to your baby's stroller, where she can reach them while she's riding. Cloth books are easy to stash in the diaper bag and can be lifesavers if your baby gets bored. Good car seat toys include Koosh balls and face cards attached to the seat with elastic or plastic links. Until your baby is at least six months old, provide only soft toys, so she won't hurt herself. Don't bring any expensive or hard-to-replace toys along when you travel, because they tend to disappear when you're out on the town. Also, skip the fancy socks and booties, if you ever want to see them again. More baby socks disappear in malls than in dryers.

Once you've assembled your supplies, wait for the right moment. If you're taking a short trip to the mall or the grocery store, plan to leave when your baby has just been fed and is fairly rested. If you're going on a longer journey, leave right before your baby's naptime so she can sleep in the car.

WHAT WILL GO WRONG

So you're all set. You've driven to the mall, popped your baby into her stroller, and you're off, towing a diaper bag big enough to hold a cow. You're ready for anything.

Wrong.

No matter how prepared you are, strange things can happen when you take an infant out in public. One friend of mine, for instance, made a quick dash into the library, only to notice simultaneously that something smelled awful, and that other library patrons were staring at him in horror. He looked down to find that his baby's diaper had catastrophically failed, and that poop was pouring out of it and down the front of his dress shirt. Another friend's infant barfed all over a display of expensive watches.

The important rule when such disasters happen is: stay calm. Most baby messes can be cleaned up with the supplies you've packed. Most store clerks are understanding. And most of the crises you'll experience are minor, and look—and smell—worse than they really are.

A messy baby can be changed in your car, or in the rest room at a mall or restaurant. Be sure to use a blanket or changing pad, and toss the blanket or pad in the laundry when you get home. A crying baby is trickier, but often a bottle or a few minutes in a quiet place will solve the problem. Also, moving your baby from her stroller to a front pack can often cheer her up; just like grown-ups, babies get tired of sitting in the same position for long periods. (They probably get tired of looking at other shoppers' butts, too.) Occasionally you may have to call the game and go home early with a fussy baby—for instance, if she won't quit squalling after fifteen or twenty minutes— but usually you'll be able to jolly her up with a backpack ride or a bottle break.

Restaurants are a little trickier, because a stinky or hollering baby will offend other diners who are spending good money on an evening out. Pick kid-friendly rather than fancy restaurants, and order something that can keep—or be prepared to get a doggie bag. Then, if your baby starts screaming, take turns walking her around outside the restaurant, or take her into the rest room until she settles down. If your baby's not too easily overstimulated, look for restaurants with balloons, colorful wall decorations, and bright lights; if you're lucky, she'll be too distracted by all the excitement to bother you while you're eating.

Grocery stores are one of the least stressful places to take an infant, because they're full of crying babies, ill-behaved children, and sympathetic moms. No matter what awful thing your baby does, she'll hardly be noticed in the general chaos. One caution, however: be careful that you don't lose any items under your baby's infant seat or

diaper bag. There's nothing more embarrassing than setting off the alarms at the front door of the grocery store
because a pot roast slid under your baby's seat and didn't
get rung up by the cashier.

If your baby is too young to sit up in the grocery cart,
carry her in a sling or pack or keep her in an infant car seat
set in the large section of the cart, rather than putting her in
the small front basket. Later, when your baby is old enough
to ride in the front of the cart, be sure to secure her in a
seat belt—I've treated dozens of children injured by nose-
dives from these carts. Another good reason to use a seat
belt: it'll keep your baby from gumming that disgusting grocery cart handle. As you shop, entertain her by keeping up a
running commentary, or demonstrating your wicked left-
handed hook shot as you toss items into your cart.

Wherever you go with your baby, she'll be happier if
you're calm, relaxed, and willing to take minor catastrophes
with humor. She'll also be happier if you can entertain her
during boring stretches—long car rides, for instance, or
while you're both waiting for Mom to try on a dozen
sweaters at the mall. Be sure to keep her supplied with toys,
snacks, and bottles, and to talk to her about the world
around her ("Look at the big truck!" "Wow—that's a great
balloon!") And if she starts looking fussy or bored, try the
exercises in this chapter, which require no special equipment and very little space, and can help you amuse and distract a baby while you're in the store or out on the town.

NOTE: *I've included activities for babies of different ages, so check
the age range at the beginning of each exercise to see if it's right
for your baby.*

"Color Commentary"

Six to Twelve Months

Years from now, your child will get plenty of stimulation at the grocery store, as she rushes around pointing wildly to those tacky, badly made trinkets in the toy aisle and shrieking, "Pleeeaaase, Dad! Pleeaase!" Or, as one six-year-old solemnly intoned to his dad, while eyeing a cheap lime green squirt gun on the toy rack, "If you buy me that, I'll never ask for anything again." Luckily, your wallet is safe for now. But because your baby is too young to care about what you're buying, she'll appreciate it if you keep her occupied with some entertaining and educational chatter while you're loading up on celery and toilet paper. This game will keep your baby amused, familiarize her with new words, make her more aware of the world around her, and stimulate her senses.

- As you shop, let your baby touch different items and talk about how they feel (crinkly macaroni, cold ice cream, etc.). If an item is lightweight, safe, and unbreakable, let her drop it into the cart. Also, give her something small and light—a box of tea bags, for instance—that she can hold while you're shopping.
- Hold up two different objects from your cart and ask your baby to look at one. For instance, hold up a box of crackers and a bunch of bananas, and say, "Where are the bananas?" When your baby looks at the bananas, say, "Yes!" and put the bananas in the cart.

GAME TIP: *Always park your cart a safe distance away from shelves and other shoppers, or you may wind up with some surprise groceries. Also, when tossing items in your cart, be sure to keep cleansers and other potentially dangerous products well out of your baby's reach.*

"Grocery Store Scores"

Six to Fifteen Months

These activities teach your baby beginning language skills, turn taking, and waiting skills. They also teach imitation, a skill she'll begin learning at around six months.

- When your baby is around ten months, encourage her to wave "hi" and "bye-bye" to each area of the store ("Bye-bye fish!" "Bye-bye cakes!").
- A couple of months later you can start to have her help you weigh fruits or vegetables on the scales, or take turns putting food in the cart. As you do, talk to your baby—for instance, "Now I'm putting apples in the

scale." (A tip: Stretch out the vowel sounds—e.g., "aaaaapples"—so your baby will hear them better.) Praise your baby if she makes a sound in response.

- While you're waiting to pay the cashier at the grocery store, make faces at your baby. Stick out your tongue, smack your lips, or blink your eyes, and see if she'll copy you. Pat your hand, and say, "Your turn!" Have a conversation: Say "da," "rrr," "oooo," or "mmmm," and wait for your baby to imitate you. When she makes a noise, repeat it back to her.

GAME TIP: *Babbling to your baby helps her learn what's called the melody of language: pitch, the natural rhythm of sounds and pauses, and patterns of loudness and softness.*

"Ready-Set-Squirt!"

Six to Fifteen Months

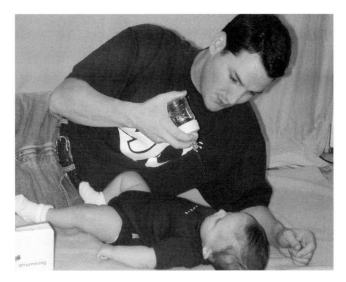

This is an excellent hot-day activity that can help prevent your baby from getting dehydrated at the park or beach. It's also helpful for a baby who's just learning to suck from a bottle. As you play this game, your baby will learn to anticipate your actions and follow you with her eyes.

- Lay your baby on her back on a blanket.
- Lying beside her, squirt a small stream of water directly into her mouth. Give her plenty of time to swallow the water, and then give her another squirt.

GAME TIP: *Be sure to aim carefully and squirt only a little water, so your baby won't choke.*

"Double Play"

Four to Fourteen Months

An endless source of amusement for babies, as well as passersby.

- As you walk through a store or mall, hold your baby up to windows or to mirrors so she can see her reflection.
- Say, "Hi baby!" and "Who's that kid?" At first, your baby won't understand that she's seeing herself and will think it's another baby. As she gets older, probably at around nine months, she'll suddenly realize: "Hey! That's me!"

GAME TIP: *For extra entertainment value, make silly faces as you and your baby look in the window or mirror.*

"Team Buddies"

Six to Twelve Months

Babies like to have something to cuddle with when they're in the grocery cart, and your little shopper will enjoy playing this grocery store game with her favorite stuffed friend.

- When you go shopping, bring a dolly, teddy bear, or other soft stuffed animal to the store with you.
- Give your baby the dolly or stuffed animal to hold as you're shopping. As you pick up food items, bring the packages to your baby and say, "Yum, yum!" and pretend to feed the dolly. When your child is old enough, she can pretend to feed the dolly or stuffed animal herself.
- Repeat with different food items, to help your baby start to register new food names.

GAME TIP: *Use a baby bungee to attach your baby's toys to the stroller.*

"Huff 'n' Puff"

Birth to Twelve Months

This is a good car game, and it's also handy for whiling away the time if you and your baby are stuck at the airport waiting for a flight. This activity helps your baby learn to pay attention, anticipate an event—she'll learn to expect the puff when she sees the tube—and become accustomed to sensory stimulation.

- Bring along a cardboard paper towel or toilet paper tube on your trip. Moving the tube like a plane, zoom in on different body parts and blow gentle puffs of air on your baby's hands, hair, and face, and on her feet and tummy if they're bare.
- Name each body part as you blow air through the tube onto it—e.g., "Here's Hannah's arm!"
- Let your baby hold the tube, and play tug-of-war with it.

GAME TIP: *Don't let your baby hold the tube for too long, or she'll drool on it and turn it into mush that she may then swallow.*

"Training Table/Ice Cube Hockey"

Eight to Twenty-Four Months

These simple restaurant games can prevent an easily bored baby from becoming fussy, and they enhance skills, including aim, balance, and turn taking.

Activity 1: Training Table

- After putting your baby in her high chair, give her a selection of crackers, Cheerios, and other finger foods you have brought along in the diaper bag. Use foods she's allowed to eat, in case she doesn't get the gist of this game right away.
- After you give your baby a bite of her dinner, say, "Now it's time to feed Daddy!" Have her give you a cracker or Cheerio and say dramatically, "YUM!" then say, "Your turn!" and give her a bite. Take turns until you're both full.
- If you're at an informal restaurant, make this game more fun for your baby by pretending to be an animal that she's feeding. Growl like a lion or quack like a duck when you're ready for another bite.

GAME TIP: *Encourage your baby to alternate her hands when she feeds you. By using both sides of her body, she'll develop symmetry. Also, if you place the food in the center of her table, you* *may get a clue as to whether she's left- or right-handed; most children express a hand preference by the time they're about eight months old.*

Activity 2: Ice Cube Hockey

- For babies between the ages of six and twelve months: Place an ice cube and a cup in front of your baby, and show her how to score a goal by putting the ice cube in the cup.
- For babies between the ages of eight and fourteen months: Place an ice cube in front of your baby and give her a straw. Show her how to hit the ice cube, using the straw as a hockey stick. Be sure to supervise her during this game, so she doesn't swallow the ice cube. You can also use oyster crackers or Cheerios.

GAME TIP: *If your baby is too young for this game, simply fish an ice cube out of your water glass and set it on her tray. Let her enjoy watching it, touching it, and seeing it melt. Again, be careful that she doesn't pick it up and swallow it.*

TIPS FOR WINNING

When things go wrong on your outings, just keep telling yourself, "This will make a funny story five years from now." Perspective is a great stress reliever.

• • •

Planning to pack your baby? If she's under five months old, use a front pack. You may need to stuff small, rolled towels or a crescent-shaped head support inside the pack to keep your baby's body straight. When your baby learns to hold her head centered and can lift it easily, she can ride in a backpack.

• • •

How can you watch your baby when she's in the backseat facing backward? Simple. Many baby stores sell mirrors that attach to the backseat, so you can see your baby's face in your rearview mirror.

• • •

Duck ponds are great places for babies. When she's old enough, your baby can help feed the ducks; until then, she'll find it hilarious just watching them.

• • •

If you're taking a long drive with your baby and you'll be changing altitudes, look for signs that pressure changes are bothering her ears. If so, give her a bottle of formula or water. Sucking will relieve the pressure in her ears. This works on airplane flights, too.

• • •

Wear old sweatshirts or T-shirts when you take your baby out. That way, if you can't get home before a poop or spit-up stain sets, it's no great loss. Also, remember that patterned shirts hide stains better than solid colors—and Hawaiian shirts offer the best stain camouflage of all.

• • •

Avoid overly ambitious trips, especially for the first few months. If you try to run more than one or two errands, you're likely to wind up with an overstimulated, screaming baby. Try to limit your outings to a half-hour to an hour.

• • •

Can you take your baby to the movies? Sure, but pick a theater with a quiet room where you can take your baby if she cries, and head for that room at the first sign of trouble. Remember, many of your fellow movie watchers are parents, too, and they've shelled out big bucks to get away from fussing and crying—so don't ruin their evenings.

THE SAFETY ZONE

Never leave your baby in the car alone while you just dash into a convenience store or dry cleaner. Always take her with you, even if she's sleeping. I treated one baby who was left in the car for just an instant, which was long enough for the car to be hit by another automobile. In other cases, parents have come out of a store to find that their cars have been stolen, with their babies still inside. And in hot weather, babies can suffer heat stroke after only a few minutes in a closed-up car.

• • •

Even if you're just driving around the block, be sure your baby is fastened securely in her car seat. A baby sitting on a parent's lap can be thrown through the windshield in an accident, or seriously injured if the parent is thrown forward.

• • •

Don't let your baby eat in a moving car. Bottles are fine, but babies can choke on solid foods if they're jostled or the car stops suddenly.

• • •

Babies can get dehydrated easily when they're outdoors—even in a swimming pool—so be sure to offer a bottle regularly.

SPECIAL PLAYS

Keep a few hand puppets and finger puppets in the car. They fold up easily and fit in the glove compartment, and you can use them to entertain your baby even if you're sitting in the front seat—as long as you're not the one who's driving! Also, leave a few toys and a pacifier in your glove compartment at all times.

• • •

Take some of your baby's favorite tapes or CDs to play while you're traveling. Also, make a tape of you or your partner singing or talking to your baby, and keep it in the car. If you're too stressed out on a long trip to make small talk, the tape will help keep your baby happy.

• • •

Spend a few dollars on toys that attach to your baby's car seat. Also, buy straps or rings to fasten toys to the seat.

They're especially handy when your baby reaches the throwing stage. Or entertain your baby by stringing toys on elastic and hanging them on a clothes hanger suspended from the clothes hook in your car, so your baby can reach them.

• • •

Make an album of your baby's favorite photos, and attach it to her seat with a short piece of elastic.

• • •

Use elastic to attach a Koosh ball to the clothes hanger on the side of the car.

• • •

Buy PlaySkool socks or wristbands, which have toys attached. Keep one set just for trips, so your baby won't get tired of them. Remember to take them off when you take your baby out of the car, so they won't get lost while you're shopping.

• • •

Pack five or six inexpensive toys in the diaper bag, and give them to your baby one at a time when she gets bored.

• • •

Sing, sing, sing! There's no better way to entertain a baby during a car ride. "Row, Row, Row Your Boat" and "Take Me Out to the Ball Game" are baby favorites, but she'll be happy even if you sing along with Smashing Pumpkins. If you're not a singer at heart, whistle or hum.

ADVICE FROM THE COACH

I hate it when people want to touch our baby at the store or the mall, especially during cold and flu season. Is there a polite way to tell them to back off?

If someone is too close for comfort, here's a neat trick that usually works and won't hurt the other person's feelings. When the admirer says, "Your baby's so cute"—they always say that—and starts to reach for her, cheerfully say, "She'll be cuter when she gets over that cold." Other people are just as worried about catching bugs as you are, and most will beat a hasty retreat if they think your darling baby is breathing germs in their direction. They may be suspicious, especially if your baby seems to be the picture of health, but they'll usually fall for it.

Also, bring antiseptic wipes along so you can give your baby a quick cleaning if she's pawed by too many admirers—especially if they're well-meaning but grimy-handed children.

I know it's stupid, but I'm mortified when my partner breast-feeds our baby in public—especially when I see people staring. Shouldn't she just bring a bottle?

The sight of mothers breast-feeding in public still embarrasses a lot of people. If your partner doesn't want to use a bottle for outings, respect her decision and help her find a quiet, out-of-the-way place to feed your baby. You can even block the view a little, by standing in front of her. And if passersby are rude, be a mensch and stick around to support her. Every time you defend your partner for making the choice to breast-feed, both she and your baby are healthier as a result.

We're broke, so I bought a used car seat at a garage sale. Is that okay?

Yes, but check to make sure that the model you purchased hasn't been recalled. You can find lists of recalled models on the Internet.

I love my baby. I love my car. My baby is destroying my car. Help!

Does your heart break every time you find spilled milk or slobbered-on Cheerios on your upholstery? If so, invest in a vinyl car seat protector. They're about seven dollars at baby stores, which is about a billion dollars less than replacing your Corinthian leather.

Also, invest in some enzyme-based spot and stain remover. To make sure it's safe, test a little on an inconspicuous area of your upholstery.

What do I do if I'm out alone with my baby, and I need to go to the bathroom?

The most important rule is that your baby's safety counts above all—including modesty. And realistically, do you think a three-month-old really cares what you're doing in there? Keep your baby in a front pack, or park your baby's stroller right next to you. Resist the urge to hand your baby off to a stranger, no matter how innocent he or she looks.

I feel like I've been reincarnated as a llama: every time we go out, my partner has me packing enough supplies to mount an expedition to the Andes. Do we really need all this stuff?

Traveling with a baby is a learn-as-you-go process. At first it's best to err on the safe side and pack too much, even if you fear you'll get a hernia. After a few months, you'll figure out what's important and what can be left at home. In the meantime, there's a third option: put bulkier supplies that you may not need (extra clothing, etc.) in the car trunk. You may have to schlep out to the parking lot occasionally, but it beats hauling those extra few pounds around all afternoon.

CHAPTER SEVEN

Surprise Moves: When Your Baby First Rolls Over

Exercises from Four to Eight Months

Parenting is a little like playing a video game, because just when you master one level, something more challenging comes along. Right now, you're about to leave level one, in which your baby stayed happily right where you put him, and enter level two, the oh-no-where-did-he-go-while-I-wasn't-watching stage.

Your growing baby is much more fun now, because he's more interactive—more attentive, more attached to you and his mom, and more curious about the world around him. By the time he's four months old, he understands that his hands and feet belong to him, and he practices using them by batting and kicking. He's learning to grasp blocks and other toys, drop toys, and rake toys toward himself with his fingers. He recognizes you by sight and smell, and he can see colors and track objects with his eyes. Every day, he's learning new skills, from saying "ooh" and "ah" to grabbing his toes. But this is a time when you'll need fast reflexes and nerves of steel, because your baby has a lust for adventure and no common sense to speak of.

The day your baby first rolls over, the lightbulb will come on over his head, and he'll say to himself, "Hey—just because he put me in this spot, that doesn't mean I have to *stay* here!" This is a Major Cognitive Event in your baby's life, and his very first step toward independence. It'll take him a few weeks to perfect the art of rolling, and still longer to perfect the art of rolling over and over and over again, but soon he'll be traveling from spot to spot, or even from room to room.

He's been preparing for this event for some time now, by strengthening his neck and tummy muscles. You've probably seen him pushing up on both arms, rocking on his tummy, shifting his weight from side to side, and swimming with his arms. All of these activities are hard work—if you don't believe it, lie on the floor and try them yourself—but they're well worth the effort, because he's been developing the strength, coordination, and motor control needed to make his first big move.

When he's only about three months old, your baby may log roll—that is, he'll turn his head, and then throw his body over in one motion as if it's a log. It's inefficient and takes a lot of effort, but he'll be excited by his achievement. He'll keep practicing until he masters the art of proper rolling—which involves moving his body in sections, bringing his arms forward and following with his legs, or vice versa—when he's somewhere between four and eight months old. He'll probably begin by rolling from his side to his tummy, although some stronger babies first roll from their tummies to their backs. That's a big project, because in order to perform a tummy-to-back roll, a baby has to lift his head, shoulders, and upper tummy, about half of his entire body weight, off the floor.

Rolling is a major milestone that changes how your baby sees his universe. Until now, he was stuck in a crib or infant seat while the world passed him by. Now he can move in two dimensions, and he'll be overcome by the urge to explore—which is why your baby's first successful attempt at rolling is your signal to baby-proof your home.

The best method? Start by getting down to floor level and looking at your house from your baby's point of view. Are there cords your baby could chew on or get tangled in? Plants he could reach and pull over? Is there junk under the couch or behind the bookcases that he could eat, or a tablecloth edge drooping temptingly near the floor? Do you have stairs he could roll down, or little rubber doorstop covers that he could pull off and swallow? Crawl around on your tummy, and imagine all of the trouble you could get into if you were him, and then eliminate any potential disasters you spot.

Remember, too, that it won't be long before your baby can stand up. Think ahead, and keep him safe by baby-proofing your cabinets and toilets with child-proof latches, removing cleansers and other dangerous products from low cabinets, putting plugs in your sockets, and removing heavy or breakable objects from low tables.

Anchor any heavy furniture or appliances that your baby could pull over, and tie drapery cords up high—they're a serious risk for strangulation—or buy cord holders at the hardware store. If you have a pool, be absolutely sure that your baby can't reach it, even by rolling. Baby-proof furniture with sharp corners by using corner pads.

Once you've made the house safe, you can focus your attention on helping your baby master his new skill of rolling. To become an accomplished roller, your baby will need good balance and coordination, and he'll need to be able to shift his weight from side to side—skills that you can help teach him by doing the exercises in this section. I've also included a tummy play activity, because your baby will need strong tummy muscles to roll over, and soon he'll also need them to sit up. Tummy play is especially important now that babies sleep on their backs. Some babies dislike being on their tummies; if yours is one of them, try putting a rolled towel or bop cushion under his chest to help support him. In addition, you'll find exercises to help enhance your baby's dexterity and fine motor skills, and even a brain teaser to give his mind a workout.

"Face-Off"

Two to Four Months

Babies love this game, which helps them bond with their dads and enhances their fine motor coordination and manual dexterity.

- Lay your baby on his side.
- Lie on your side, facing your baby.
- Place your baby's hand on your cheek, and let him feel your stubble.
- Rub his hand gently over your face and say, "You're giving Daddy a shave!"
- Rub his hand gently over your hair, and say, "You're combing Daddy's hair!"

- Identify parts of your face—for instance, "You've got Daddy's nose!" "That's Daddy's lip!"
- Switch sides, so your baby can play this game with his other hand.

GAME TIP: *As you talk to your baby, emphasize new words you want him to learn—"This is Daddy's NOSE!"*

"Teddy Bear Tackle"

Three to Six Months

The goals of this exercise are to encourage your baby to reach forward independently, and to help him initiate rolling. Also, side lying is a very important transitional position between lying down and sitting.

- Lay your baby on his side.
- Lie on your side, facing your baby.
- Place a big stuffed teddy bear between you, close enough so your child can reach it with his hand.
- Say, "Bear! Grrrrr!" Encourage your baby to reach for the bear. As he becomes proficient at this, move the

bear farther away so he'll need to reach across the midline of his body to touch it.

• Switch sides, so your baby can play this game with his other hand.

GAME TIP: *To keep your baby's interest, use different stuffed toys.*

"Towel Turnovers"

Three to Six Months

The stability provided by the towel in this exercise will help your baby practice his back-to-side roll without being startled. In addition, this exercise will work on graded movement—that is, your baby's ability to make slow, gradual position changes.

- Wrap your baby gently in a towel, as shown.
- Gently roll him from his back to either side.

GAME TIP: *Never leave your baby unsupervised in the towel. If he falls asleep, remove the towel.*

"Place Kick II"

Three to Six Months

Successful rolling requires lots of leg action. When you do this activity with your baby, he'll learn to lift his legs and roll them toward the side—a motion similar to the movement he'll use when rolling over.

- Place your baby in his infant chair.
- Hold a balloon within kicking range of his feet. At first, keep the balloon straight above his feet. Let him enjoy kicking the balloon with his toes.
- Next, move the balloon to the left. In order to kick the balloon, your baby will need to reach his leg to the left. After he's kicked the balloon several times, switch sides so he can practice with the other leg.

GAME TIP: *Never leave your baby unattended with a balloon— especially one that is popped or hasn't been blown up! An unexpanded balloon or a popped balloon can suffocate a baby.*

"Traveling"

Two and a Half to Six Months

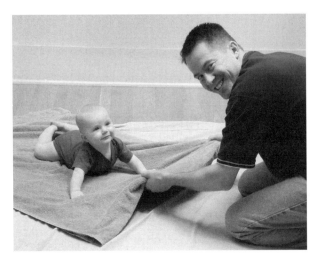

Here's another tummy builder. It'll also help your baby learn to shift his weight from front to back and from side to side, improve his balance, and teach him to lift his head and push up in preparation for crawling.

- Put your baby tummy-down on a quilt or blanket on the floor. Be sure he can hold his head up and breathe easily.
- Slowly pull the blanket forward, backward, or sideways, saying, "Here we go!" Be careful to make your moves smooth and gentle, so your baby will have time to adjust.

GAME TIP: *If your baby needs additional support to do this exercise successfully, place a rolled-up towel or a bop cushion under his chest.*

"Roller Derby 1"

Four to Eight Months

Here's an excellent activity for prerollers who are able to hold their heads up and centered. It'll work your baby's tummy muscles, and enhance his coordination and balance.

- Lay your baby on his tummy across your lap as shown. Holding him firmly but gently, lift your chest so that he rolls to the side. Keep your movements slow, and keep your baby's arms forward.

GAME TIP: *Larger babies are often slower to roll than other infants, simply because they have to lift more weight against gravity.*

"Roller Derby II"

Four to Twelve Months

Help your baby learn to hold his head, neck, and back in alignment as you take him on a flight with Dad. He'll also learn to keep his arms forward, and to use his eyes to fix on a point—in this case, your face—for stability.

- Lie on your back, with a pillow under your head.
- Holding your baby firmly under his arms, lift him off your chest and fly him forward and back, and from side to side, making airplane noises as you move him. Make your movements slow and gradual.

GAME TIP: *As your baby gains confidence, gradually move him a little faster.*

"Road Trip"

Three to Six Months

While you're touring the house together, your baby will be learning to open his hands; developing arm and shoulder strength and stability; and practicing protective extension—the art of moving his arms down and forward to prevent himself from bumping his head or nose. This skill will help protect him from injury later, when he learns to sit.

- Stand, holding your baby as shown.
- Zoom your baby to different locations—for instance, a table, a chair, or the back of the sofa.
- As you reach each new spot, encourage your baby to put his hands down on the surface to take his weight on his arms.

GAME TIP: *Hold your baby firmly and provide support to his arms and elbows, so he doesn't bump his head.*

"Tot Yacht"

Three to Six Months

Although your baby can't sit alone yet, he's grown-up enough to test the waters—especially if he does it safely, as in this exercise. It develops back, neck, and shoulder stability, and helps your baby become more independent.

- Drape a towel inside a laundry basket big enough for your baby to sit in.
- Put your baby in the basket, positioning him as shown.
- Keep the basket still at first, and let your baby enjoy sitting up as you read him a story or play together with a toy. As he becomes more comfortable, move the basket slightly.

GAME TIP: *Provide additional padding if your baby needs extra support or seems anxious.*

"Ping Pong Challenge"

Four to Six Months

Most moms can't stand to watch their babies become frustrated. Dads are better at letting babies figure things out for themselves, which helps them gain self-confidence—a quality that games such as this one can foster. It also helps your baby learn about the concept of object permanence, an idea that babies at the rolling stage are ready to understand.

- Place your baby in his infant seat, and sit on the floor, facing him. Let him watch you while you place a Ping-Pong ball or other small object in one hand. Then close your hand around the ball so it can't be seen.
- Ask your baby, "Where's the ball?" Encourage him to look at your hand, or, if he's old enough, to point to it. Don't show him the ball right away; instead, let him think it over. When he looks at the hand where the ball is, show it to him and say, "Yay!"
- Put the ball in your other hand, and repeat the game.
- Next, place the ball under a cloth, leaving part of the ball visible. Ask your baby, "Where's the ball?" Encourage him to look by patting the ball or making a zooming noise as you move your finger toward it.

GAME TIP: *When your baby's around eight months old, hide the ball completely under a blanket or in a shirt pocket.*

TIPS FOR WINNING

Most babies start teething between four and eight months. You'll know when that first tooth is on the way, because your baby will fuss, cry, drool, and stick every available object in his mouth. Ease his suffering a little by chilling his favorite chewable toys in the fridge (not the freezer); the coolness will help numb his gums. Also, try giving him a cold, wet washcloth to chew on.

•   •   •

By the time your baby is about four months old he'll discover that splashing in the pool or tub is great fun. Bear with him, and even encourage him, because he's toning his arm muscles each time he drenches you.

•   •   •

To help your baby learn balance, eye-hand coordination, and other skills, buy him an Exersaucer with toys attached. A good Exersaucer is a little pricey, but it's worth its weight in gold because it'll keep your baby happily and safely busy while you do chores or read the paper.

•   •   •

A little tickling is okay, but be careful not to overdo it! Watch your baby; if he turns blotchy or starts fussing, stop right away. Remember, after a few seconds, tickling stops being fun and starts being torture.

•   •   •

Infant thermometers are a controversial topic. Hospitals and doctors' offices use ear thermometers all the time, but research indicates that they're not very accurate: in one study, the researchers found differences of up to four degrees between right- and left-ear measurements. Armpit thermometers, too, are convenient but less than perfect. If you decide to use an ear or armpit thermometer, keep the rectal thermometer on hand for those occasions when you need a highly accurate reading. Unfortunately, it's still the gold standard for temperature taking.

P.S. If you buy an ear thermometer, ask your pediatrician when it's okay to start using it. Some doctors want you to wait until your baby is more than a year old, so there's less risk of damaging the ear canal.

THE SAFETY ZONE

Is it a good idea to rub whiskey on the gums of a teething baby? Doctors differ, but the consensus seems to be: probably not. Over-the-counter teething gels are a better idea, but be sure to buy brands designed for babies. Adult brands can numb your baby's mouth and throat, creating a choking risk. Avoid two other popular teething-pain remedies—Popsicles and frozen bananas—because babies can bite off pieces big enough to cause choking.

• • •

Babies at the rolling stage get stuck easily. If you need to leave the room for more than a few seconds, pop your baby in his playpen or crib to keep him safe. Also, babies at this stage love to burrow, so keep quilts, pillows, sleeping bags, and shopping bags safely stored away.

• • •

Your baby's hands are more open now, and he'll enjoy raking the carpet with his fingers to capture threads, sticks, hair, or anything else he can stick in his mouth—so be sure to vacuum frequently!

· · ·

Never shake your baby or toss him in the air. Even when it's done as a game, it can cause shaken baby or shaken child syndrome, a condition that occurs when a baby's or a toddler's head is whiplashed back and forth. Even mild shaking can cause subtle brain damage, while forceful shaking can result in seizures, vision loss, mental retardation, or paralysis.

SPECIAL PLAYS

Blow bubbles for your baby. If you get tired of this activity before he does, hold the bubble wand in front of a fan and make bubbles the lazy way.

· · ·

Challenge your baby by placing toys just slightly out of his reach. He'll stretch both his body and his mind by solving this intriguing problem.

· · ·

Wait for a moment when your baby is talkative, and tape him babbling. Then play it back to him later. Some babies are real hams and can't get enough of hearing themselves! Make a new tape every few weeks, as he learns new sounds.

· · ·

An empty oatmeal box cylinder makes a great toy. Put it on its side, and show your baby how to pat it and roll it.

Also, put a toy inside the oatmeal box, ask your baby, "Where's the toy?" and pull it out.

• • •

Help your baby learn to localize sounds by holding up a squeaky toy and moving it slowly from side to side while squeaking it occasionally. When your baby's older, about six months, hide the squeaky toy under a blanket, squeak it surreptitiously, and ask, "Where's the toy?"

• • •

A four- to eight-month-old baby is ready to take an active part in reading games. Buy books with different textures, and books with built-in flaps or finger puppets, and look for books that show only one item per page—for instance, a ball or a car. Encourage your baby to look at the pictures by asking, "Where's kitty?" "Where's house?" By now, he can eye point—that is, he can make a choice between two objects or pictures by turning his eyes to the correct one.

• • •

Make a video of your baby playing with you, and play it back for him.

ADVICE FROM THE COACH

There's hair on my four-month-old's sheets. I know baldness runs in my family, but this is ridiculous—can my baby really be losing his hair?

Yes, but don't reach for the minoxidil. The downy hair a baby has at birth starts falling out around now, but it's being replaced by grown-up hair. Most parents don't notice this change, because the new hair is growing in while the old hair is falling out. The new hair, by the way, may be a different color than the baby fuzz, so don't be surprised if your redhead turns into a blond or a brunette.

By the way, your baby's eyes will probably change color, too. If you're African-American, Hispanic, or Asian, your baby may have been born with hazel eyes; if so, you'll probably notice that his eyes start to become a darker brown around five or six months. If you're Caucasian, your baby probably started out with blue eyes that are just now starting to show their true color.

Our friends' infant is much louder and more demanding than our baby. Why are our babies so different, when they're the same age?

By the time babies are three or four months old, they start revealing their true personalities: some are show-offs, some are shy, some are content and quiet, some love people and smile at every new face, and some are hard to please. It sounds like your baby is one of the happy, easy-going types, so count your blessings! But don't count on it happening twice. It's a funny law of life that hardly any-body gets two easy babies, so if you have another child, your next one may be a doozy.

I do recommend that babies who are markedly dif-ferent from other infants—extremely fussy, unusually quiet, etc.—receive a thorough hearing, speech, and devel-opmental evaluation, just as a precaution. However, you're likely to find that your baby, whether he's a little whirl-wind, a placid soul, or a fusser, is exhibiting perfectly normal personality traits.

Our baby does some activities repetitively—for instance, he'll bat at the same toy on his crib gym dozens of times. Why?

Did you ever practice the same golf stroke a hundred times, or spend hours trying to make the same three-point shot in basketball? Your baby can be just as obsessive, because to him, successfully batting an object is just like sinking a three-pointer or hitting the sweet spot on a golf ball. He'll practice batting and other new skills repetitively, and in the process, he'll build important neural pathways in his brain. In particular, he'll be learning to integrate the input from different senses when he repeatedly touches a colorful toy, jiggles a musical ball, or sticks a rattle in his mouth.

Are pacifiers okay? My mom says our son will have buckteeth if we let him suck on a pacifier all day. My partner says she'll go insane if we take it away from him.

Three topics that are virtually guaranteed to start an argument are politics, religion, and pacifiers. Proponents say that pacifiers are the only way to survive your baby's fussy periods. Opponents say they'll ruin your baby's mouth. I side with the pacifier users, and so does the American Academy of Pediatric Dentistry. "Most children stop sucking on thumbs, pacifiers, or other objects on their own between two and four years of age," the Academy says, "and no harm is done to their teeth or jaws." Of course, if your son does develop buckteeth, your mother will never stop saying "I told you so." But that's a risk worth taking, if it saves your partner's sanity—and yours.

My partner says she's ready to get back to our Saturday-night dinner-and-a-movie routine, but I'm nervous about turning our six-month-old baby over to a sitter. Isn't she too young to be left with a stranger?

Even parents who haven't watched *The Hand That Rocks the Cradle* are nervous about leaving their children with sitters, at first. You'll feel better, however, if you follow these simple rules for selecting and testing a sitter:

- Until your child is one year old, never use a sitter who's less than twelve years old. Even when your child is a toddler, avoid using young teens as sitters unless they're mature for their age and have had extensive experience caring for babies.
- Insist on references. Even if you're hiring a neighborhood teen, ask for the names of other parents for whom he or she has worked.
- If you use a regular sitter, occasionally come home earlier than expected. When you pull this trick, however, pay the sitter for the extra hours—unless you catch her hitting the gin bottle or making out with her boyfriend on your sofa. Another ploy is to duck in, after you've been gone for an hour or so, and say you need to pick up something you've forgotten.
- Ask a friend or neighbor to drop in once in a while, and do a little casual spying: "Oh, sorry, I didn't know they weren't home. I just needed to borrow a cup of sugar. How are you and the baby getting along—and where exactly did you get that tattoo?"
- Try to find a sitter who's taken a Red Cross baby-sitting course or has similar training. You might even

offer to pay your sitter to take a CPR, first aid, or baby-sitting class.

- Should you consider video surveillance? It's a controversial issue, because sitters feel, with reason, that it's an invasion of their privacy. However, spying on your sitter is legal, and a few parents have indeed discovered, by using hidden cameras, that the Mary Poppins look-alikes they hired turned into abusive creeps when they weren't around. If you do install a surveillance camera, think about telling your sitter up front that he or she is being monitored.

- Above all, trust your gut. If anything about a potential sitter worries you, find a different one. You won't have any fun when you're out on the town if 90 percent of your brain cells are busy worrying about what's going on at home.

CHAPTER EIGHT

Major League Milestone: When Your Baby Sits Up

Exercises from Five to Nine Months

In every game, there's an ultimate test. In basketball it's the three-pointer—or, if you're Shaquille O'Neal, the free throw. For golfers, it's mastering that long drive down the fairway, or hitting the ball out of deep rough. In karate, it's breaking a stack of boards. But in the game of babyhood, there's an even tougher skill to master, and that's sitting up.

For a grown-up, of course, sitting is easy. In fact, most of us wish we could do it more often, preferably in front of the TV with a cold drink and a bag of Doritos. To a baby, however, sitting up is a daunting challenge that requires months of training. In fact, it's far more difficult than rolling, crawling, or even walking.

To find out why, lie on the floor on your back or stomach and, starting from either position, sit upright. Make your movements as slow as you can, so you can feel each muscle working. Notice how every part of your body, from your head and neck to your shoulders, arms, stomach, back, and legs, gets into the act. Then, once you're sitting up, have someone give you a little shove, and notice how many muscles you use to catch yourself and keep from tipping over.

Clearly, there's a lot more to sitting than meets the eye. Remember, too, that as adults, we're usually sitting *down* from a standing position. Getting *up* into a sitting position, as a baby does, is much harder, because it takes a series of well-timed movements of muscles, all working together at just the right time and at just the right speed. It's scary to boot, because your little one will have a lot of tumbles before she masters the art of staying upright.

Fortunately, your baby is up to the challenge. She's spent months lifting her head and shoulders against gravity and learning to support herself on her arms. She's discovered how to shift her weight by rocking and swimming on her tummy. By now, too, she can hold her head firmly upright, and roll from her tummy to her back and from her back to her tummy. When all of these skills are in place, your baby is ready to put them together and master the art of sitting upright.

Be prepared, however, to watch your baby keel over any number of times while she learns to sit. Be sure she's on a carpeted surface when she tries! She'll be scared and frustrated, but let her work through it. Instead of becoming alarmed when she tips over, make cheerful and encouraging small talk, so she'll realize that an occasional spill is no big deal. Each time she practices, she'll get better both at sitting up and at *staying* up once she's in position.

Initially your baby will learn to sit up when she's placed in a sitting position, a skill she'll master at around five or six months. Then, at eight months or so, comes the really hard part: learning to get into and out of sitting. This requires a high degree of coordination, balance, and muscle strength. In addition, your baby needs to develop what's called protective extension—that is, her arms must come forward or out to her sides to catch her if she starts to tip over. I've included several exercises in this chapter that work on protective extension, because it is a skill your baby will need to protect herself from head injuries when she sits and, later, when she stands and walks.

NEW SKILLS, NEW FEARS

Your six-month-old baby will spend much of her time grasping and holding her toys—a pastime that will teach her volumes about spatial relationships (up, down, in, out, inside, outside, beside, between, behind, under) and spatial orientation. For instance, she can now tell if a toy is upside down or the right way up. She also loves pat-a-cake, and she enjoys peekaboo games because she understands object permanence.

One thing your six-month-old *doesn't* enjoy is seeing Mom or Dad leave. That's because she's old enough now to experience separation anxiety, the intense fear of being apart from you. She can also tell the difference between familiar faces and strange ones, and she's likely to be afraid of new people. In fact, if your job requires lots of travel, you're likely to notice that your baby is a little frightened of *you* when you return from a trip. Try not to take it personally; the older she gets, the less of a problem this will be. In the meantime, be sure Mom has plenty of photos or videos of you with your baby, so she can look at your face even if you're miles away. Also, spend lots of time playing with your baby when you're home, so she'll know for certain that you're an important guy.

While you're spending time with your baby, work on teaching her to use a cup and a spoon. It's tempting to stick with the bottle as long as possible, because it's *so* much less messy. But switching your baby from a bottle to a cup helps prevent tooth decay and lets her practice using both hands together. It also provides a workout for the lip and tongue muscles that she'll soon need to make *p*, *m*, and *b* sounds. In short, the benefits are worth mopping up a few extra oatmeal and prune juice disasters. For some mess-free practice, also give your baby a spoon and cup to play with in the tub.

You can help your baby develop oral skills, and practice her sitting-up skills as well, by doing the exercises in this chapter. Because your baby is soaking up new words right now, be sure to keep up the chatter while you work out together.

"Blanket Coverage"

Five to nine Months

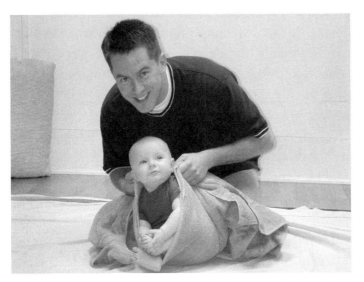

While she's snug and secure in her blankie, your baby can practice her sitting balance and learn to adjust to sideways motion.

- Place your baby in a blanket as shown, being sure that she's securely enclosed, and that her back is straight and well supported. Let her enjoy the sensation of sitting up while being protected from falling by the blanket.
- As she becomes more secure in the blanket, gently move it so your baby leans slightly to the left or right.

GAME TIP: *Do this activity only if your baby is at least four months old.*

"Hang Time"

Five to Eight Months

Triceps need a little toning? Then try this exercise, which in addition to building your own muscles, will strengthen your baby's back and legs, preparing her to sit and stand with a straight back later on. Also works on your baby's balance skills.

- Holding your baby in one palm, slowly lift her above your head. If your baby is too large for you to do this easily, use two hands.
- Repeat several times.

GAME TIP: *Be sure you have a firm grip on your baby before lifting her!*

"Pick-Up Game"

Five to Eight Months

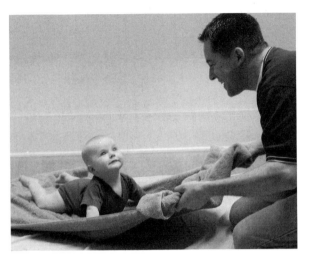

A fun floor game that helps your baby develop speedy reactions, and teaches her to make corrections when her balance is upset.

- Place your baby on a blanket as shown.
- Grasping two corners of the blanket, lift the corners so your baby is lifted slightly off the ground.
- As your baby learns to maintain her center of gravity and keep her balance, begin to move the blanket very slowly and carefully.

GAME TIP: *Do this exercise only if your baby is able to hold her head up well and can stay on her tummy comfortably for at least a few minutes.*

"Defensive Moves I"

Five to Eight Months

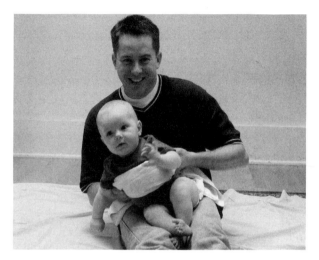

Give your baby a mini–roller coaster ride with this simple activity. It'll help her learn to shift her weight from side to side, and bring her arms out to protect herself.

- Sit as shown, with your baby in your lap. Hold a towel around your baby's tummy, grasping it with both hands.
- Gently roll from side to side, using the towel to stabilize your baby. Be sure your baby returns to a centered position each time, so she learns the sensation of sitting upright.

GAME TIP: *Make very slight movements at first, and roll farther as your baby becomes more confident.*

"Defensive Moves II"

Six to Ten Months

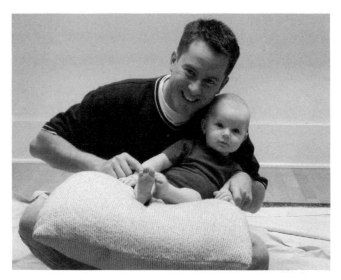

This is a little more advanced than the previous exercise, because there's no towel to offer extra support for your baby's tummy.

- Place your baby on a pillow on your lap, as shown.
- Gently rock your baby from side to side, using your arms to stabilize her.
- Always return her to a centered position before rocking to the side again.

GAME TIP: *Leaning to one side or the other can be a little intimidating for your baby at first. Be sure you encircle her snugly, to offer her a sense of security.*

"On the Ball"

Six to Ten Months

Your baby will get a kick out of feeling so tall as she sits up on the ball in this exercise. As it shifts underneath her, she'll develop stability and learn to balance and shift her weight in response.

- Place your baby on a ball about the size of the one shown in the picture.
- Hold your baby securely, sitting close enough so that she can touch your face.
- Slowly lift one of your baby's legs, bending her knee one to two inches and causing the ball to shift slightly. Then straighten the leg by extending your baby's knee. Alternate legs, being sure to move the ball only

slightly so she doesn't fall backward or sideways but instead learns to maintain control and stay centered. Always bring your baby back to a centered sitting position before moving the ball again.

GAME TIP: *This activity helps your baby learn to maintain her balance if she begins to fall to either side, or forward or backward, as she's learning to sit. It also teaches her to come back to the center if her equilibrium is upset.*

"Daddy Surfboard"

Six to Twenty-Four Months

Can life get much cozier than this? Your baby will enjoy lying comfortably on your back, and she'll be refining her balance and developing a strong back.

- Lie on a well-padded floor, resting on your elbows.
- Have your partner place your baby on your back.
- Very gently and slowly move your hips one to two inches, shifting your weight to one side. This will let your baby experience the sensation of moving her weight from one side of her body to the other side while remaining centered and balanced on your back.
- Have your partner remove your baby when you're done.

GAME TIP: *Be sure not to move suddenly while you're doing this activity.*

"Rug Rat Races"

Six to Twenty-Four Months

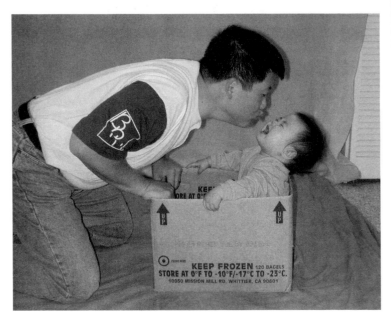

In a few years, your child will be begging you for a Power Wheels sports car. Right now, fortunately, she'll happily settle for a low-tech cardboard box. This driving exercise, designed for babies already able to hold their heads up, will help her develop good sitting balance, and teach her to shift her weight easily.

- Place your baby, sitting up, in a laundry basket or cardboard box. For smaller babies, use a smaller oval basket and add towels for extra support. The basket should be large enough for her to sit in comfortably, but it should be cozy enough that she can reach the sides easily to balance herself. Use a quilt or pillows to keep her snug and secure.

- Put the box on your lap.
- Move the box from side to side using your legs, and make "Vroom! Vroom!" noises.
- Put the box on the floor, and push or pull it gently around the house.

GAME TIP: *If your baby has a set of plastic keys, show her how to start the engine by shaking the keys or turning them at the side of the box. Also, pretend to fasten your baby's seat belt, stop at the gas station for a fill-up, etc.*

"Ball Handler"

Five to Twelve Months

Helps your baby learn to shift her weight forward and backward, and teaches her to use her arms to prevent herself from falling.

- On a carpeted floor, place your baby in front of you, in a sitting position. Put a large ball in front of her, as shown.
- Encourage your baby to hold the ball and push against it. Be sure to stay close, to offer support.

GAME TIP: *The larger the ball, the more support it will provide to a baby who's just learning to sit up.*

"Riding High"

Six to Twelve Months

While she's way up on Dad's shoulders, your baby will be exploring spatial relationships and improving her balance and equilibrium.

- While sitting on the sofa, place your child on your shoulders. Do not stand up. She'll love the new perspective on her world.
- For added entertainment, do this activity while sitting in a sturdy chair in front of a mirror or window.

GAME TIP: *Do this activity only if your baby or toddler is able to push up over her arms on her tummy and hold her head up well. This could be dangerous for babies who haven't yet developed some sitting balance, or whose heads are still wobbly.*

"Pep Talk"

Six Months and Up

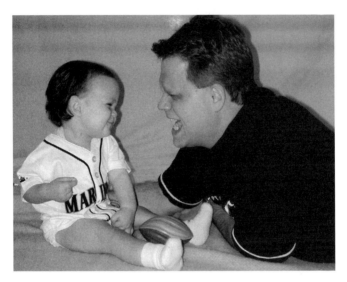

Babies at the sitting stage love to learn new words and behaviors by imitating their parents. This activity will help your baby practice speech sounds, and it may encourage her to say "Da-Da" a little sooner!

- Sit, on the floor or couch, facing your baby.
- Say, "Give me an 'Ooooo.' " Praise her and clap if she makes any sound in response.
- Repeat with "Wooo," "Waaaa," "Aaaa," "Mmmm," "Nnnnn," and, of course, "Da."

GAME TIP: *Babies learn to say vowels first. Next they learn prolonged vowels (ah, ooh, eee), and finally consonants.*

TIPS FOR WINNING

Once your baby is fairly confident at sitting, challenge her by placing toys just slightly out of her reach. When she leans to grab them, she'll be improving her balance.

• • •

Now is a good time to buy a full-length mirror, if you don't already own one. Your baby will enjoy admiring herself, and patting her reflection in the mirror.

• • •

Start a coming-home routine: when you come in the door, say hello to your baby by name, and give her a big smile and a tummy raspberry or a kiss. She'll associate your arrival with fun, and you'll find that the big smile you'll get in return is a great stress reducer after a tough day on the job.

• • •

Tired of picking up the toys your toddler tosses? Buy her some that attach with suction cups to her high chair.

• • •

Pushing your baby to sit, crawl, or stand before she's ready won't speed up her overall development. In fact, it may undermine your baby's confidence and possibly make her slower to try new activities. I know it's frustrating when your best friend's baby can sit or stand weeks before yours does, but parenting is not a competitive sport.

• • •

When you read to your baby, emphasize and prolong the initial sounds of familiar words—"Ddddddaddy," "bbbb-ball." This helps your baby learn to differentiate between sounds.

177

THE SAFETY ZONE

When you're buying baby paraphernalia, pass on the baby walkers or bouncers. They're dangerous and can actually make it harder for babies to master the tummy, head, and arm control they need to learn to walk. A recent study found that babies placed in walkers were slower to sit up, crawl, and walk, *and* slower to develop mentally, than babies whose parents didn't use walkers.[3] They can also cause fractures and head injuries if babies tip over in them.

• • •

Do you have floor lamps in any of your rooms? If so, be sure they're placed safely so that your baby can't pull them over.

• • •

Keep the number for your local Poison Control Center taped to the fridge or the inside of a kitchen cabinet.

• • •

Tempted to prop your baby on the sofa and dash off to answer the door or the phone? Wait until she's able to sit well—otherwise, she might take a nosedive while you're gone.

SPECIAL PLAYS

Put a straw in a glass of water, and blow air through it. Your baby will get a big hoot out of the burbling noise and the bubbles you'll generate.

• • •

[3.] Siegel, Andrea C., and Burton, Roger V. Volume 20, pages 355–361. *Journal of Developmental Pediatrics.* October 1999.

Nesting toys help a six- to eight-month-old learn about sizes, shapes, and spatial relationships. Augment your baby's store-bought nesting toys with plastic measuring cups, and mixing bowls of different sizes.

• • •

This is a great age for pots, pans, and spoons. Vary your baby's selection by giving her both metal and wooden spoons, and offering different sizes and shapes of pans.

• • •

Give your baby a mini-lesson in physics by letting her throw and drop different types of objects. She'll learn, for instance, that a soft rag moves through the air differently from a foam ball or a stuffed animal.

• • •

Your baby loves to hear her name, and by now she'll respond when you call her. Insert her name in some of her favorite songs, and use it when you're playing turn-taking games. "Now it's Hannah's turn!"

• • •

One of the best ways to help your baby learn to sit confidently is simply to play ball. Sitting about two feet from your baby, roll a ball to her and encourage her to roll it back. Be sure to give her a cheer when she catches or pushes the ball, and say, "Touchdown!"

ADVICE FROM THE COACH

We'd finally gotten our baby to sleep all night long. Now she's starting to wake up again during the night. Why?

For one thing, she may be experiencing teething pain.

If so, ask your pediatrician about giving her liquid Tylenol before bedtime. Also, now that she's more mobile, she's likely to roll over or even sit up when teething pain or a wet diaper awakens her during the night. Once she's fully alert as a result of this activity, it may be hard for her to fall asleep again. Remember, too, that the sitting-up age is also the separation anxiety age, and babies at this stage can be frightened if they awaken and don't see Mom or Dad.

A diaper change, a cool teething ring, and a quick cuddle will usually solve the problem, and allow you to get back to bed without losing more than a little sleep. Be careful not to give your little insomniac too much attention, however, or she'll think that this middle-of-the-night routine should become a habit.

Can listening to Mozart really make my baby smarter?

Hard to say. Some researchers believe that listening to classical music builds babies' attention skills and mathematical ability, while other researchers think that's baloney. To date, there's no good research to support the "Mozart Effect." And as a friend of mine said, after reading a book about the boorish composer, "If listening to Mozart makes you smart, how come it didn't work for him?"

It's certain, however, that listening to a variety of musical styles—particularly the complex structures of classical music—will stimulate new pathways in your baby's brain. And classical music can be soothing and stimulating. Sleepy babies love Bach and Mozart, while one friend's baby loved to boogie to "Carmina Burana."

Should we brush our baby's teeth?

Yes, because it'll get her used to the routine of brushing her teeth early on. You can either rub her gums with a soft cloth, or use a very soft baby toothbrush that fits over your finger (available at baby stores or drugstores). Don't use toothpaste or cleaning gels; plain water is just fine.

My partner nurses our baby to sleep each night, and again when she wakes up at night. Is this bad for our baby's teeth? Will it make her overly dependent?

This is something you and your partner should discuss. Some people feel that their babies need to reconnect by nursing at night. Others believe that by the time babies learn to sit, their digestive systems are mature enough, and their tummy capacity is large enough, that they can go for six hours without nursing. There's no right or wrong answer, but you both should feel comfortable with the nighttime feeding plan.

If your partner does decide to nurse your baby at night, one of you should wipe her teeth afterward with gauze. Otherwise, the sugar in the milk might cause tooth decay.

My partner's mother thinks we should start feeding our baby solids—but our baby doesn't like them, and she spits them out.

Most experts suggest holding off on solids until your baby is old enough to sit independently. When you do start feeding solid foods, be patient, because a baby experiencing her first cereal or bananas is as hesitant as you were the first time you visited a sushi bar or tasted escargot. Expect some messes at first, while your baby is learning to tolerate the taste, smell, and feel of solid foods.

CHAPTER NINE

Up and Running! Your Baby Masters Crawling and Standing, and— Finally—Takes That First Step

Exercises from Six to Eighteen Months

You've anticipated the Big Moment for months. The camera's loaded with film, and the video recorder is ready to roll. But don't be surprised if you arrive home one day soon and hear your partner or your baby-sitter say, "Guess who took his first steps today!"

It's a fact of life that babies almost always choose to start walking on a day when Dad's out earning a living or getting the tires rotated on the car. But don't feel too bad if you missed the event, because your baby will want to show off his new skill for you, and he'll be just as delighted the tenth time as the first. And keep the camera and the video recorder ready just in case, because you might get lucky. A few babies *have* been known to take their first steps while their proud Papas are on hand to watch.

CRAWLING: IT'S IMPORTANT!

Before your baby walks, of course, he'll need to master two other skills: crawling and standing. Contrary to what you may have read, the first is an important milestone that shouldn't be skipped.

I know that many baby books tell you it doesn't matter if your baby doesn't crawl. And indeed, many babies never crawl, instead scooting on their bottoms or simply going from sitting directly to walking. However, babies who do learn to crawl develop strong and stable shoulders and arms. They also develop fine motor coordination, important for everything from playing a musical instrument to painting and writing. And crawling helps integrate both sides of the brain, which fosters academic skills, including reading, writing, and math.

So give your baby lots of floor time so he can practice the skills he'll need to crawl. If he belly-crawls like a Marine rather than lifting his tummy off the floor, help him refine his technique. And if he doesn't try to crawl by the time he's nine or ten months old, the "Four-Point Stance" exercise in this chapter will give him a jump start. Try them, too, if your baby skipped the crawling stage and is already walking.

FROM CRAWLING TO CRUISING TO STEPPING OUT

It doesn't take long for a crawler to start pulling up and standing. Before your baby takes that first step, he'll practice for weeks, first by standing when he's placed against a table, and then by cruising around tables and walking with support from Mom or Dad.

When your baby first learns to stand, he'll be enormously proud of himself—until he gets tired and tries to sit back down. Unfortunately, it's a *long* way down from his point of view. Sitting back down is harder than standing up, because it requires more controlled movement, so don't be surprised if you find your baby standing at your coffee table, crying as if the world's coming to an end. Gently help him to back down, so he doesn't get frustrated. Eventually, once he learns to bend his knees and hips and sit down slowly, he'll find standing a thrill.

At that point, your baby will start cruising sideways, using tables or chairs for support and balance. As he does, he'll learn to shift his weight, and to stand on one foot at a time—both prerequisites for independent walking. At some point, probably between nine and twenty months, he'll let go of the table, the chair, or a grown-up's hand, and take that first tentative step or two all by himself. Once he does, there's no stopping him.

OUCH!

Babies at the crawling, standing, and walking stages are busy learning other skills, too, including reaching for anything close to them. You'll find this out the hard way because anything, from your nose to your dog's tail, will suddenly be fair game. Women wearing dangling earrings and teens with nose rings are favorite targets as well— something to consider when you're interviewing baby-sitters! This new interest in grabbing stems from the fact that your baby's fine-tuning his thumb-and-first-finger pincer grasp, and can now reach his arms forward easily.

When he's not causing you bodily injury by grabbing your ears or poking at your eyes, your baby may be busy trying to climb everything in sight. It's a skill he needs to practice, but preferably not on your entertainment center or your potted ficus. If you have room, build him a climbing area using old cushions and a child cube chair, or put a baby slide in the family room, so he'll have a safe challenge to tackle. Use baby gates to keep your baby off the stairs when you're not watching him—and, when you can supervise him, let him practice climbing stairs and teach him to crawl down backward. It's much easier and safer than going headfirst.

FIRST WORDS

Your baby is also learning his first new words and will delight you by saying "ba" for "ball" or "bot" for "bottle." In addition, he's learning to understand and use gestures, so teach him to point when he wants a toy or a treat. Read to him every day, and you'll help him start to build a big vocabulary. Right now he'll love repetitive rhyming books, push-button books, and books that play songs. And talk, talk, talk. It doesn't matter if he doesn't have a clue what you're talking about; he'll be mesmerized by the tremendous importance of whatever you're telling him, and he'll be picking up new words and even learning rudimentary grammar. Use single words or short phrases—"big potty!" "soft kitty"—so he'll comprehend more of what you say.

One warning, however, about your baby's increasing communication skills: in just a few months, he'll be able to repeat any short words you use, and he'll be especially attracted to the very words you don't want him to learn. This can lead to enormous embarrassment, especially when the grandparents come to visit: "No, I'm sure he said 'fork.' Really." So now is a good time to get out of the habit of swearing, at least when your baby is within earshot.

In the meantime, work on skills that *will* impress the grandparents. The exercises in this chapter will help your baby learn everything from masterly crawling and walking to cognitive and social skills, and they'll give him a positive outlet for his energy and curiosity.

Pillow Peekaboo

Six to Sixteen Months

Babies love this exciting game, which teaches them object permanence (the concept that people or objects still exist, even when you can't see them) and helps them take their first steps toward separation from their parents.

For babies six to nine months old:

- Place your baby on a bed, sitting up. Surround him with large, soft pillows so he's hiding inside a little pillow cave.
- Encourage your baby to push the pillows away, and when he does, say, "Peekaboo!"

For babies eight months old and up:

- Place your baby on the bed, on his tummy. Place a small, lightweight pillow touching his head, arranging it so it will fall away if he raises his body.
- Encourage your baby to push up on his arms, knocking the pillow away, or to move from his tummy to a sitting position and push the pillow away. When he does, say, "Peekaboo!"

GAME TIP: *Do the second part of this exercise only if your baby is comfortable on his tummy. Be sure to supervise your baby at all times during this activity.*

"Four-Point Stance"

Eight to Twelve Months; your baby must be able to sit up

Does your baby do a belly crawl, with his tummy staying on the floor? If so, this simple exercise can help him learn to crawl effortlessly. This exercise should be done on a carpeted floor, or—if you have hardwood floors—on a blanket or a quilt.

- Put your baby on the floor, tummy down. Place a mid-size towel, folded lengthwise, around his chest, directly below his shoulders. Be sure the towel is under his chest, not under his tummy.
- Grasping the ends of the towel with your hands, raise your baby to a crawling position while you stand over him.

- Very slowly, rock your baby forward and backward, using the towel to keep his chest off the floor. This will teach him to shift his weight comfortably, and help him build arm and leg strength and coordination.
- Gently pull one end of the towel forward while pulling the other end backward, simulating a crawling motion.
- As your baby gets better at balancing when you do this exercise, encourage him to crawl while you support him with the towel.

GAME TIP: *If your baby's legs splay out during this exercise, put your feet on either side of his knees to offer extra support.*

"Rodeo Rider I"

Eight to Sixteen Months

This classic favorite works on side-to-side balance skills, timing, and your baby's ability to use his upper and lower body together.

- Position yourself on the floor, supporting yourself on your knees and elbows.
- Have Mom place your baby on your back.
- Gently move from side to side. Make your movements very slow.
- As your baby gains confidence, try lifting one arm so your baby will need to shift his weight slightly.
- When your baby's balance and strength improve, give him a horsey ride by moving forward very slowly.

GAME TIP: *Do this exercise on a soft, carpeted surface.*

"Rodeo Rider II"

Eight to Fourteen Months

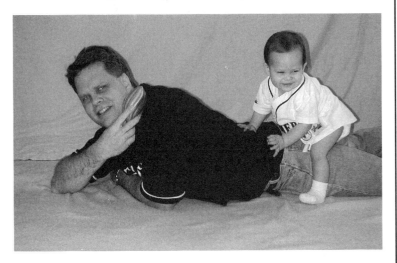

This exercise helps your baby learn to relax his hips and bend them so he can sit down and stand up. In particular, it helps him develop the hip stability and graded hip movements he'll need to move slowly into the sitting position, instead of going kersplat.

- Lie on your front on the floor.
- Have Mom place your baby so that he's straddling one of your legs.
- Lift your hip, to help your baby stand.
- Relax your hip, to help your baby sit.

GAME TIP: *To add to your baby's fun, roll a ball down your back toward him (see photo).*

"Racing Form"

Eight to Fifteen Months

"**W**ow—I'm standing up all by myself!" Your baby will be tickled by this chance to show off his new ability, and he'll enjoy having an opportunity to stand independently without worrying about falling, because the towel will keep him upright. This activity will help him gain the confidence he'll need to stand without holding on to Mom's or Dad's hand. In addition, he'll be able to practice jumping for the first time while Dad holds him safely and securely.

- Kneeling behind your baby, place him in a standing position and wrap a towel around his chest as shown. Be sure to hold it firmly, so he won't wobble.

- As you support your baby with the towel, encourage him to stand up. Be sure his legs are straight and his bottom is tucked in.
- When he can do this, provide less and less support until he is standing independently and the towel is no longer supporting his weight.
- Next, use the towel to lift your baby so he experiences the feeling of leaving the floor and then landing again. Gradually he'll learn to bend and straighten his legs in order to jump.

GAME TIP: *Watch your baby's feet. If they're turned out, place your own feet outside of his as guides.*

"Big Bopper"

nine to Sixteen Months

A sturdy bop is a reassuring thing to cling to when you're just learning to stand on your own two feet. As your baby stands against the bop, he'll be learning to balance and shift his weight forward. He'll also be developing strong shoulders and arms, reinforcing his protective extension skills, and gaining confidence in preparation for independent standing.

- Place the bop on a carpeted surface.
- Stand your baby on one side of the bop, using your sofa for additional support (see photo).

- Check your baby's foot alignment. His feet should be pointing forward, not in or out.
- Sit on the other side of the bop. As you're sitting, slowly move from side to side, playing "peekaboo" with your baby. Be careful not to move the bop—just peek around it.
- As your baby becomes more confident and his balance improves, gently move the bop in the direction of the sofa. Eventually your baby will let go of the bop and stand alone.

GAME TIP: *Air-filled bops are available for $10 to $20 at most toy stores.*

"Take a Hike"

nine to Sixteen Months

If you thought plungers were only for sinks, think again! Here's a plunger exercise that will entertain your baby and teach him new skills at the same time. The plunger walking sticks provide stability and balance, promoting independent standing and helping your child learn to step forward and make the transition from standing to walking.

- Have quarter-inch dowels cut to two inches above your child's height. Cover their tops with rubber tips, and stick rubber plungers to their bases.

ROOKIE DAD

- Place your baby in a standing position, with his feet a shoulder width apart. Place the outer borders of your child's feet near the plunger bases. Make sure his bottom is tucked in and not sticking out; you can use your knee to support his back and bottom in the correct position if necessary.
- Place your baby's hands on the sticks. Put your hands over his to provide support, and let him practice standing.
- Once your baby gains confidence, practice walking slowly while using the sticks for balance.

GAME TIP: *Your baby should make reciprocal movements when he walks with the sticks; that is, when he moves his left arm forward he should move his right leg forward, and vice versa.*

"Instant Replay"

Five to Twenty-Four Months

Remember when you used to torture your friends by repeating everything they said? Unlike them, your baby will love this game—and it will encourage him to increase his babbling. How soon will that babbling turn into real words? At five to seven months, your baby will say "da" and other single syllables; at seven to nine months, he'll be able to say "da-da-da" and other multisyllabic sounds; and by the time he's ten to eighteen months old, he'll be trying out real words such as "Daddy" and "dog."

- Sit on the floor, facing your baby.
- Wait patiently for him to say something. Then repeat it back, exactly as he said it.

- Be perfectly quiet until he says something else. Again, repeat whatever he says. Try different intonations—a high voice, a low voice, etc. Eventually, he'll get the joke, and make more and more noises to see if you'll repeat him.

GAME TIP: *By the age of nine months, babies listen much longer to words said in their own language than to words spoken in other languages. The more you talk to your baby, the better he'll recognize the sounds and speech patterns of his native tongue.*

"Fancy Footwork"

Ten to Twenty-Four Months

You have some mighty big Nikes to fill, but your baby's up to the task. Kids love this activity, which promotes balance skills and helps give them the self-confidence they need to stand independently.

- Place your child in a pair of your shoes, as shown. Be sure the distance between the shoes doesn't exceed your baby's shoulder width.
- Provide support while your baby stands, making sure he's secure. If he wants to take one step forward or back, offer assistance.

GAME TIP: *If you're using shoes with laces, tie the laces up so they don't drag on the floor.*

"Bike Racer"

Twelve to Twenty-Four Months

Promotes independent standing, improves balance and self-coordination, and helps your baby learn the transition from sitting to standing.

- This exercise should be done on a soft carpet. You'll need a baby bike with a narrow seat, not more than twelve inches wide or tall, with a twenty-four-inch handle on the back. The bike should be the right size for your baby to be able to push it comfortably and walk with it, and it should have a beeping bell or horn.

- Place your baby in a sitting position on the bicycle seat. Push him around slowly, to help him learn to balance.
- Next, stand your baby up and encourage him to sit back down on the bike.
- Teach your baby to move the bike independently by giving the bike one push and then encouraging him to use his feet to move it.
- Once your baby has mastered moving the bike in a sitting position, help him stand and push the toy while you keep your hands over his to ensure that the bike doesn't move forward too fast. When he is comfortable doing this, remove your hands from his and let him stand independently while holding on to the bike. Keep the bike still at this stage, so it doesn't move while he's standing.
- Next, let your child try walking while holding the handle for support. Be sure you hold the bike to keep it stable.

GAME TIP: *You can buy a bicycle toy for $15 to $50, depending on whether it's wooden, plastic, or metal.*

TIPS FOR WINNING

By the time your baby is crawling, he'll begin coming to you for comfort or assistance. When he does, drop whatever you're doing and lend him a hand. When you do, you'll let him know early on that Dad's a smart, helpful, reliable guy he can turn to when he has problems in life.

• • •

One of the best investments you can make when your baby starts walking is a lock for your VCR door. It costs about $5 and can save you about $300 in repair costs—and you'll also avoid the heart-stopping experience of peeking in the VCR door and discovering that missing slice of French toast. If you have trouble finding a VCR lock at your local hardware or baby store, try the Internet.

• • •

Looking for a way to entertain your baby while you're at home alone together? Wait until he's especially talkative, and then call up Grandma and Grandpa and let him have a conversation. He'll enjoy hearing voices on the other end of the phone, and you'll make your parents' day, too.

• • •

If you buy your baby a toy TV remote, a toy cell phone that lights up and makes noises, and some big plastic car keys, then he'll be more likely to leave your real toys alone.

• • •

Babies at the crawling stage often have trouble staying still. If your baby fights you when you put him in the car seat, or tries to wiggle free when you're changing his diaper, try distracting him with a musical toy or a rattle.

THE SAFETY ZONE

Have you seen those teach-your-baby-to-swim books and videos? Forget it. Contrary to what some experts will tell you, a baby isn't ready to swim under water. Babies can swallow dangerous amounts of water if you try to teach them to swim, so hold off on underwater swimming until your child is at least three.

• • •

Don't let friends or family members smoke around your baby. If you don't want to offend them, put an ashtray and a comfortable chair and table outdoors for them. And never let anyone leave cigarettes or lighters within your baby's reach.

• • •

Also be careful not to leave alcoholic drinks where your baby can reach them. It's amazing how a baby who's barely able to hold a training cup can suck down a scotch and water, given the chance. And scotch, unfortunately, looks a lot like apple juice to a little person.

• • •

If you live in earthquake country, fasten all of your tall furniture to the walls. Remember that even a cabinet that's shorter than you are could seriously injure a baby if it fell on him during a quake. In fact, fastening heavy bookcases and chests to your walls is a good idea even if you're not in an earthquake-prone area, because babies love to climb and can pull furniture over on themselves.

• • •

If you toss sodas or beer in a big tub of ice for parties, be sure to drain the tub as the ice melts. Better yet, put the

205

tub where your toddler can't get to it. Also be careful with buckets of car-washing water.

. . .

Now that your baby is constantly on the move, you'll have to put some extra thought into holiday decorating. If you get a Christmas tree, buy a small, wide tree and put it in a sturdy base. Cut off all lower branches, use unbreakable ornaments, keep light strands off the bottom third of the tree, and do your best to find a spot for the tree that's not too accessible to your baby. Also, if you light candles for Hanukkah, Kwanza, or Christmas, be aware that a curious baby might try to climb a bookcase or coffee table to grab them. Instead, put candles on a high, sturdy table, and don't leave your baby unsupervised when the candles are lit.

. . .

Keep your knife drawer locked, put a cover over your stove dials, and place your coffeepot well away from the counter edge.

. . .

Pad the corners of your coffee table and fireplace hearth.

SPECIAL PLAYS

Now's the time to buy a good set of wooden, foam, or cardboard blocks. Stack them up and let your baby knock them over. He can do this over and over without getting bored, and you can play this game while keeping one eye on the Cowboys and 49ers. He'll also enjoy banging the blocks together, and when he's somewhere around nine to twelve months old, he'll learn to stack them as well.

•   •   •

Let your baby try finger painting with whipped cream or yogurt. He'll make a mess of his high chair, but you can hose it down outside.

•   •   •

By the time your baby is nine or ten months old, he'll begin to understand slapstick humor. Dads are usually way better at this than moms, probably because they watch more reruns of *The Three Stooges*. Entertain your baby by doing gorilla imitations, wiggling your fingers in your ears, or generally just acting silly. Your partner may not approve, but your baby will think you're amazing. One of your baby's first attempts at humor, by the way, will be to offer you a toy or a cookie and then snatch it away. This joke is a perennial favorite with the under-one crowd.

•   •   •

Believe it or not, your one-year-old is ready to start working on computer skills. He's a little young for Sim City or Railroad Tycoon, of course, but he can learn to play his first computer games. Jump Start Toddler, Reader Rabbit Baby, and Reader Rabbit Toddler are great pro-grams for toddlers, and even eight- to twelve-month-olds are grown-up enough to enjoy them with help from Dad. One suggestion: if you upgrade to a new computer, save the old one for your baby; then you won't have to worry about mashed bananas on your own keyboard.

ADVICE FROM THE COACH

I love bike riding. Is a baby carrier that attaches to my bike safe for my eight-month-old to ride in?

No! The National Bicycle Helmet Safety Institute says, "Nobody we have met in the injury prevention field recommends taking an infant of less than twelve months in a bicycle child seat, trailer, sidecar or any other carrier. Nobody. And we do not either."

In fact, the experts at the Institute aren't keen on bicycle carriers for babies of any age. They note that bike-mounted carriers place your baby's weight above the center of gravity of your bike, making it more difficult to control. Moreover, they say, "Parents often have no idea how many jolts and shocks are delivered to the child's body in a normal, slow, careful bike ride." A trailer that attaches behind your bike may be less likely to cause accidents than a bike-mounted carrier, but it's still a rough ride—and given new findings about shaken baby syndrome, some experts worry that babies who ride in trailers or bike carriers may suffer subtle brain damage. And, of course, babies of any age can be injured or killed in a crash, or seriously hurt if a bike falls over.

My recommendation? Take the money you were going to spend on a bike carrier, put it in the bank, and use it in ten years to buy your child a Mongoose BMX. He'll appreciate it far more than the headache you may give him if you haul him around in a bike carrier now.

My baby hates vegetables. This worries me, because I've read all of the reports about the importance of fruits and vegetables for good health. What should I do?

Feed vegetables at the beginning of a meal, when your child is most hungry. Most kids have one vegetable they like; keep offering it, or try blending it with other vegetables. Add grated cheese, if your child likes it. Also, offer veggies in small, enticing containers. Save those teriyaki, soy sauce, or tartar sauce containers you are given with fast-food orders, because they make great baby-size bowls.

Many kids like fresh fruit or vegetables better than the squashed ones in jars. Try frozen peas—just one or two to start—frozen raspberries or green beans, or a fruit kebab of bananas and berries on a straw.

More importantly, don't force-feed your baby vegetables. Instead, offer two bites, and let him make up his mind whether he wants more or not. He'll eventually find some veggies he likes, and he won't be unhealthy in the meantime.

One more idea: give your baby a spoon to hold and bang while you're feeding him. He may be so amused that you can sneak in a few bites of squash or carrots without getting it spit back in your face.

My eleven-month-old recently developed an intense fear of water. He used to love taking baths, but now he screams bloody murder when it's tub time. What's going on?

It's not uncommon for babies to develop bath phobia, either early on like your son, or in their toddler years. Don't worry, because it's almost always a brief phase. Here are some tricks that might help him overcome his fear:

- Buy special bath toys and a music tape that you play only during bath times. Try to find a tape with happy songs about water ("Rubber Duckie," etc.).

- If your baby became fearful of bathing shortly after he graduated from an infant tub to the big tub, let him go back to a baby tub. If it's okay with him, set the little tub inside the big tub. One smart dad whose baby was too big for the infant tub solved the problem by putting his baby in a laundry basket inside the big tub. Some babies feel much safer confined in a small area than sitting in a huge bathtub.

- Run the bathwater before you bring your baby into the bathroom, so the noise won't scare him. Also, leave the water in the tub until he's out of the bathroom. Young babies may dislike the noise of a draining tub, while older babies sometimes become completely convinced that they're going to be whooshed down the drain along with the water!

CHAPTER TEN

A Whole New Ball Game: When Your Baby Turns One

Exercises from Six Months Upward

If you just blew out the candle on your baby's first birthday cake, congratulations—you're about to begin a whole new adventure called toddlerhood.

Now that your baby has reached the one-year milestone, she'll change, grow, and learn so quickly that you'll have difficulty keeping up. Over the next few years, as she moves from infancy to childhood, you'll experience new joys—from the thrill when she first says "Hi, Daddy," to the triumph when she learns to eat with a spoon or sinks a two-pointer with her Nerf basketball. In addition, you'll face new challenges, from tantrums to tears, and you'll experience the mixture of pride and trepidation that comes with watching your little one become more and more autonomous.

How can you help your baby make the most of this crucial transitional period? By starting right now to give your one-year-old a head start on the academic, social, and life skills she'll need to succeed.

EARLY LEARNING: HELPING YOUR BABY MAKE THE GRADE

It's a well-known fact that intelligent Dads usually have intelligent kids, which means that the next Einstein could be sitting on your study floor emptying your bookshelves right now. But when it comes to smarts, genes aren't everything. Nurture is just as important as nature, and you can actually give even the brightest toddler a boost in the learning department by providing plenty of brain exercise in the form of new experiences.

Your child's brain is currently under construction. Over the next two years, trillions of connections will form between her brain cells, and those connections will help determine everything from how well she'll speak a foreign language to how good she'll be at trigonometry, history, or quantum physics. Every interesting new experience you offer her—petting a goat, smelling a flower, reading a new book—will build new connections, and those connections translate into increased brainpower.

The more you teach your baby today, the better off she'll be when she sets foot in the classroom. That doesn't mean, however, that you need to teach your baby to add and subtract, or read letters, or point to pictures on flash cards. The current fad is to push children into learning faster and faster—"Your baby can learn math at one! Your child can read Proust at three!"—but I don't recommend boring your child to tears with classroom-style academics. You won't really give her a head start, because she's not ready developmentally to comprehend first grade math or read sentences. And ask yourself this: when you look back on your life, do you say, "Gee, I wish I'd spent more time with flash cards?"

My advice is to forget the workbooks and drills, and use your home and your neighborhood as your classroom. Give your baby a nature lesson, for instance, by letting her help you plant a garden. In the kitchen, show her how to make instant pudding; in the bathroom, flush the toilet and let her watch the water swirl down. Introduce her to the ants and earthworms in your backyard, and water the yard together so she can learn how water comes out of the hose. Show her how bathtub toys float, and how rocks dropped into a puddle sink. Make it your goal to introduce her to at least one new and fascinating idea or activity every day.

Also, get down and dirty with your child every once in a while. Dads are usually better at this than moms are, because they worry less about laundry stains and grubby hands. Give your child a mini-lesson in geography by building mud rivers and mountains together—or teach her about different shapes by making sand castles, using a variety of cups, bowls, square food containers, toilet paper tubes, and pails to mold your masterpieces. She may not be too good at building sand creations yet, but you'll find that she's an expert at smashing them.

NO TIME? NO PROBLEM!

If you're one of those lucky dads who's home every night and every weekend, it won't be hard to find opportunities to teach your child about her world. But if you're so swamped with overtime work or other obligations that you don't have time to make Play-Doh snakes, build Duplo houses, or take your child to the zoo, you can still give your toddler's brain cells a workout, even if you can only spare ten or fifteen minutes at bedtime. How? Just by picking up a book. Reading is one of the most important learning activities you can share with your child, because children who are read to have larger vocabularies and do better in school than other children. So, if your work schedule allows, start a bedtime-story reading ritual with your baby. In addition to teaching her new words and exposing her to new worlds, a cuddle with Dad and a bedtime-story session at the same time each night will relax her and help her fall asleep—which means that you might even get a chance to read a book of your own!

As you read, involve your baby in the story. Ask her to point to pictures, or to turn the pages. Also, don't argue if your baby wants to read her favorite books over and over and over again. Your brain may recoil at the idea of reading *Goodnight Moon* for the 167th time, but a familiar book is as great a joy to your child as that well-worn tape of *Terminator II* is to you.

LIFE SKILLS: HELPING YOUR BABY BECOME INDEPENDENT

As a newborn, your child depended on you for everything. As she grew older, she took her first steps toward autonomy by learning to sleep alone and to comfort herself when she was upset. Now she's eager—in fact, determined—to do more and more tasks independently, because she wants to be all grown up, just like you. While it's frustrating to watch her drop her toys when she's trying to clean up, or spill Cheerios all over the table when she's mastering eating with a spoon, it's important to help her become a capable little person.

Interestingly, this is one area in which men tend to outshine women. Because moms have a low tolerance for frustration or unhappiness in their children, they have a strong urge to jump in and say, "Let me help you" or "I'll do it for you" or "Don't worry, Mommy's here." Dads, who often have a more realistic view of what children need to know in order to survive, are more willing to stand back and say, "Okay, kid, give it your best shot."

Of course, your toddler won't master grown-up skills all at once, so help her out by breaking tasks down into doable parts. A one-year-old can clean up one or two toys by herself, for instance, but don't expect her to straighten up a big mess.

It's equally important not to be too critical if your child's first attempts at independence fall far short of perfection. When she eats with a spoon, expect lots of spills, a messy chin, and no table manners whatsoever. If she wants to put her hat on by herself, let her—even if she puts it on backward. In each case, let her do what she can by herself, say, "That's wonderful!" and then tactfully finish the job yourself. At this stage, it's important to praise the attempt, rather than judge the outcome.

One way to ease your child's transition to self-sufficiency is to make her first steps toward independence as easy as possible. If your child is trying to master using a spoon, for instance, feed her easy-to-capture foods such as mashed potatoes. Give her a big toy box so it'll be easy for her to clean up her playtime messes, and provide structure for this task by helping out—"You put in a toy, and then Daddy will put in a toy." Also, give her plenty of opportunities to make simple choices—for instance, "Which book do you want to read?" or "What do you want for lunch?"

SOCIALIZATION 101: HELPING YOUR BABY SUCCEED AT THE GAME OF LIFE

As your baby grows into toddlerhood, she'll develop a mind of her own. On the bright side, this means that she'll be more fun, imaginative, and assertive—more her own little person. On the other hand, it also means that her behavior may sometimes be a challenge.

As your child grows older, the things that drive you crazy when she's a baby—crying, refusing to sleep, pinching, yelling—may give way to tantrums, hitting, kicking, and ignoring your instructions. It's not easy, even if you're the wisest of dads, to know what to do at these times. How should you react when your child throws her Tippee cup on the floor? What should you do if she pulls the dog's tail, or kicks the other children in her play group? And more importantly, over the long run, how do you help your child learn the rules that will help her lead a successful life? The first step, before you worry about your child's behavior, is to define your own.

We've all known fathers whose idea of parenting was to ignore their children until a disaster occurred and then holler, spank, and punish. Maybe you were raised by one yourself. In fact, fathers used to be largely relegated to the roles of breadwinner and disciplinarian. But times have changed, and that change is a healthy one for both dads and their kids.

Why? Because drill sergeant dads can do long-term damage to their relationships with their children—and studies show, compellingly, that the yell-and-spank approach to parenting does more harm than good. In fact, research by Harvard psychiatrist Michael Commons shows that parenting practices that cause stress in babies can actually change the children's brains, raising their levels of the stress-generated biochemical cortisol and possibly making them more susceptible to personality disorders later in life.[4]

In addition to being counterproductive, the drill sergeant approach simply isn't necessary. Because my job involves working with hundreds of infants and toddlers, I've seen more than my share of tantrums, hitting, spitting, biting, and screaming. And it's possible to handle it all—without spanking, yelling, or threatening.

So instead of visualizing yourself as a drill sergeant— "You WILL BEHAVE, young lady!"—think of yourself as a head coach whose job is to shape winning behavior. While your short-term goal may be to handle a tantrum, or stop your child from biting the cat, your long-term goal is to teach her how to be a good person for life—and that

---

[4.] Research by Michael Commons reported at the 1998 meeting of the American Association for the Advancement of Science. See "Stressed Babies May Be Prone to Trouble Later," Maggie Fox, Reuters News Service.

means praising, guiding, and directing her. It also means being patient, because social skills are challenging for even the most obliging young children to understand. It means being creative and innovative, and seeking new, positive ways to help your child learn these life skills. And when behavior issues arise, it means responding in a logical, loving, consistent manner—creating a learning experience, rather than a battleground. If you can establish a pattern of consistent and gentle guidance right now, your child is likely to reward you—and herself—by becoming a happy, well-adjusted person who's a joy to be around.

SOME DO'S AND DON'TS

There's no one right or wrong way to help your child learn the skills of social behavior, because every child and every parent is different. However, some time-tested strategies should be part of any good game plan. Here, based on twenty years of dealing with babies, are my best recommendations:

Avoid the word "no." Many parents wear out this word—which is why you hear so many young children yelling "No! No! No!" right back at Mom and Dad. Instead, try using words that will give your child some insight into the reason why her behavior concerns you. For instance, teach your child, early on, to understand the meaning of the words "hot," "ouch," "stop," "danger." If your child is reaching for a hot stove, say "hot"; if she's running into traffic, say "danger."

Eliminate disasters waiting to happen. Babies are naturally impulsive, often clumsy, and very "high energy," so try to avoid situations in which your child will get into trouble through no fault of her own. Put breakables or other items you don't want her to touch up high, or in the closet. Keep your briefcase locked, put your cell phone where your child can't reach it, use TV and VCR locks, and block off taboo areas whenever possible.

Make transitions less stressful. Many behavior challenges occur during transitions—for instance, at bedtime, or when it's time to leave the park. You can help avoid tears or arguments by preparing your child for these changes. For instance, say, "We'll be leaving the park in a few minutes," or "Bedtime soon!" If a sitter is arriving, let your child know well ahead of time, and give her a photo of you and Mom to hold while you're gone.

Try distraction or redirection. If your child is jumping on the furniture or tossing your books off the shelves, distract her with another activity. Suggest a walk or a snack, or say, "Hey, look, there's the postman—let's go get the mail!" Or redirect her: if she's banging on your glass-topped coffee table with her shoe, steer her toward her toy workbench and hammer, or give her an oatmeal box and some wooden spoons to use as drumsticks. Babies have the attention spans of Spice Girls fans, and sometimes this works to your advantage.

Don't have unrealistic expectations. Your child will frequently spill food, make messes, or have accidents simply because she's too young to control her behavior in an adult way. She's impulsive, overwhelmingly curious, and often unaware of dangers. It's your job to educate her, and help her learn to control her impulses, but it's a long-term job—so don't frustrate yourself or her by expecting instant results.

Set a good example. Your child will look to you as a role model, so act the way you want her to act. If you stomp and scream and curse every time things go wrong, you'll teach her that tantrums are the right way to handle problems. Conversely, if you model mature, unselfish, and self-controlled behavior, she'll be more likely to exhibit good behavior herself.

These are all good guidelines for helping your child learn how to behave in a manner that will make both her and you happy. But again, the most important point to remember is simply that you and your child are on the same team. Whatever approach you use, make it clear to your child that you have high expectations because you love her.

As you and your baby head into the new adventure of the toddler years, it's more important than ever to stay close and let her know you're an important part of her life. The following exercises, which focus on both cognitive and physical skills, are a fun way to help your baby learn and refine her new grown-up skills, while the two of you share time and strengthen your relationship.

"Baby Bowl Game"

Eight to Twenty-Four Months

What can a fishbowl teach your child? Plenty, including sorting and categorizing, fine motor skills, dexterity, skillful grasping and releasing, and refined hand movements.

- Use a clean plastic fishbowl, available for $10 to $12 at stores. Alternatively, you can use an oatmeal box or a milk carton.
- Give your baby balls, plastic animals, or other objects to place in the fishbowl and then remove. Have her place one object in, and remove one.

GAME TIP: *As your child grows older, challenge her during this game by placing several objects in the bowl and telling her which one to catch.*

"Hole in One"

Eight to Twenty-Four Months

Here's a favorite brainteaser which teaches memory skills, listening skills and vocabulary, fine motor coordination, and grasping and releasing skills.

- You'll need a toilet paper tube or paper towel tube for this activity, as well as some small toys. Sit your baby on your lap. Hold the tube in your hand where she can reach one of the openings. Hand your baby a small toy, and tell her to put it in the tube.
- Ask, "Where did it go?" Give her plenty of time to solve this mystery; she'll enjoy puzzling it out.
- Gradually add several toys to this game.

GAME TIP: *Supervise your baby at all times during this activity, to make sure she doesn't swallow the toys.*

"Halftime Band"

Ten Months and Upward

Give your little learner an early lesson in music appreciation, while teaching her how to use a tool—in this case, the xylophone stick—to achieve a goal. She'll also be working on refined hand movements, graded arm movements, and listening skills.

- You'll need a toy xylophone for this exercise.
- Encourage your baby to play the xylophone, and teach her the concept of "soft" and "loud."

GAME TIP: *No xylophone? Make one of your own, by filling plastic water glasses with different levels of colored water and letting your child tap them with a wooden spoon. Be sure to use sturdy glasses, and be prepared for a few spills!*

"Blocking Basics"

nine Months and Upward

Stacking them, whacking them, building with them: there's no end to the fun that your baby can have with a simple set of blocks. In the process, she'll be learning important engineering skills and improving her eye-hand coordination.

- Put a block down, help your baby pick another one up, and guide her as she places it on top of the first one.
- When she's done stacking blocks, have fun knocking them down together.

•Alternatively, build a ramp with the blocks. Encourage your baby to roll a toy car, ball, doll, or other object down the ramp.

GAME TIP: *Avoid the game of bopping yourself or your baby on the head with the blocks, even if you do it gently. That's a habit you won't want your baby to form, especially since she's not yet very practiced at hitting softly.*

"Sports Page II"

Six to Thirty-Six Months

Does your toddler crawl all over you while you're trying to read the Sunday sports section? If so, make checking the stats a family affair.

- Let your baby sit in your lap as you read the sports section.
- Point out photos—e.g., "There's Kobe Bryant making a basket!" "Look at that horse—he won the race!"

GAME TIP: *Let your baby take the lead in this game sometimes by encouraging her to point to pictures and then telling her about them.*

"Volleyball Star"

Eight to Thirty-Six Months

This activity promotes visual attention, develops your child's eye-hand coordination and motor accuracy, and works on balance and timing.

- For this activity, you'll need a ball attached to a piece of elastic. You can find these at almost any toy store.
- Place your baby or toddler in a sitting position against Dad's tummy, for support.
- Give your child the ball, and say, "Go ball." When your baby releases the ball, let her track its movement with her eyes.
- Encourage your child to hit the ball. If she's over one, encourage her to hit it several times in a row.

GAME TIP: *Be careful not to leave your baby unsupervised with this toy.*

"Budding Ballplayer"
Ten Months and Upward

Looking for an activity that takes only a few minutes and works on everything from visual attention and eye tracking to spatial concepts and eye-hand coordination? Try this simple but educational ball game.

- Hold your baby as shown. With your other hand, hold a ball within her reach.
- Move the ball, and ask your baby where it is. Encourage her to look for it and touch it.
- Try moving the ball in different directions: up and down, side to side, round and round.

GAME TIP: *You can also use beanbags with these activities.*

"Half-Pint Hoopster"

Ten to Thirty-Six Months

It's never too early to practice basketball skills! As your child shoots for the hoop, he'll be increasing his arm strength and learning to make controlled movements to direct his throws. He'll also learn frustration tolerance as he keeps trying to make baskets, and he'll learn goal-directed behavior.

- Use a foam ball. If you don't have a toddler-size hoop, use a trash can or cardboard box.
- Show your child how to make an overhand shot toward the basket.
- Praise all attempts—"Good try," "Almost got it," "Nice shot!"

GAME TIP: *As your child gets good at this game, encourage her to gradually move farther away from the basket.*

"Reading with Daddy"

Here's my recommended reading list for babies.

- *Three to six months:* Plastic books, photo books of daddy and baby together, singing books, books with repetitive sounds and words (e.g., *Goodnight Moon*)
- *Six to nine months:* Cardboard books with holes, doors, and flaps that open.
- *Nine to twelve months:* Books with pictures of familiar objects to build vocabulary, small push-button books (three to four buttons), books with contrasting textures (e.g., *Pat the Bunny, Farmland*).

TIPS FOR WINNING

Observe what interests your one-year-old intellectually and follow her lead. For instance, if she's fascinated by birds, buy a bird feeder and help her sprinkle birdseed in it every day. If she likes to make music, pick up a triangle, some maracas, or a harmonica. A budding mechanic? Buy her a toy workbench and tools.

• • •

Educational supply stores aren't just for teachers. These stores are wonderful sources of toddler treasures including mind-stretching games, books, and toys. They're also great places to take a toddler, because almost everything in them is unbreakable.

• • •

Beware of creating learned helplessness in your child. If you habitually take over tasks your child is struggling to complete, you'll teach him the wrong lesson: "I'm not very competent. I can't do things by myself. I need help." If you need to, sit on your hands—literally!—to keep yourself from reaching out instinctively to lend a hand when it isn't really needed.

• • •

Hell hath no fury like a toddler whose TV gets turned off in midcartoon. However, you'll do your child a favor by strictly limiting her TV and video-watching time, because research shows that children are nearly five times as likely to be overweight if they watch more than five hours of TV per day than they are if they watch little or no television.

THE SAFETY ZONE

Many medicines look like candy to kids. Keep medications locked away in high cabinets, and teach your toddler that bottles labeled with "Mr. Yuk" stickers (frowny-face stickers that are available at most drugstores) aren't candy and could make her sick. When you give your child medicine, be sure to call it just that—medicine—rather than suggesting that it tastes delicious. Also keep vitamin/mineral supplements out of reach: there's enough iron in many of them to be deadly, if a child swallows a bottleful.

• • •

If you ever reach the point where you find yourself losing control during one of your child's tantrums, don't stay in the room. Instead, just walk away. Even the most saintly parent reaches the breaking point once or twice, so don't feel guilty. Just remove yourself from the situation until you've simmered down and it's safe to return.

• • •

Reserve a special tone of voice for talking about safety matters. That way, you'll get your child's attention quickly if she's about to do something dangerous.

SPECIAL PLAYS

Play classical music, show tunes, or jazz at dinnertime. It'll put everyone in a mellow mood and help your child develop an ear for good music.

. . .

While your one-year-old is much too young to learn addition or subtraction, you can incorporate counting into her games. Count "one, two, three!" as she jumps, or count her blocks as she stacks them up. As she hears you count out loud, she'll begin to learn the names of numbers.

. . .

Make personalized books for your child, using photos and stories about her pets, family members, trips, special events, or even everyday activities. Or, if you're into computers, create "virtual" books and post them on your toddler's very own Web site.

. . .

Help your child learn to categorize objects by sorting objects—for instance, foods, books, cars, and animals.

. . .

Weary of watching your child bounce off the walls, or listening to her fuss or cry? Buy her a drum, a toy workbench, and other toys she can pound on, so she'll have positive outlets for her energy, frustration, or aggression. Just as adults release frustration by taking a long run or doing an hour of Tae-Bo, children need to let off steam in physical ways.

. . .

Correct your child's behavior when necessary, but don't hold a grudge. No matter how difficult she was today, let her start off tomorrow with a clean slate.

233

ADVICE FROM THE COACH

Our one-year-old likes to listen to books on tape. Can I play these for her at bedtime?

Story tapes have their place, but they're no substitute for a warm, cuddly, interactive Dad. A tape won't stop to explain a word your toddler doesn't know, or read the best parts over again, or laugh along at the funny parts. It's okay to supplement story reading with tapes, but your toddler will get far more enjoyment and mental stimulation when you perform live.

My baby cries when it's time to leave the park, or turn off her video at bedtime. What should I do?

Help her articulate her feelings by saying, "You're angry." When it's time to put her video away, reassure her, "We'll put it right here for next time." Also, give her a concrete object to serve as a memento of what she's missing; for instance, if she's crying when she leaves Grandma's house, give her a small toy or trinket from her home—or if she's upset about leaving the park, pick up a rock or stick and say, "We'll take a piece of the park home with us."

Our friends brought their one-year-old to our house a few weeks ago, and our child fussed and cried the whole time. Why?

The green-eyed-monster can raise its head even at an early age. Your child can't articulate her feelings, but she's jealous when she sees you acting gaga over someone else's baby or toddler. When similar situations arise in the future, try to focus on both children—and reassure your daughter by saying "Daddy loves you," if you hold the other child.

I was a pudgy, out-of-shape kid, and it took me years to get in shape. How can I instill the fitness habit in my child early on?

No sweat! Your one-year-old will enjoy simple games and activities such as playing catch, kicking a ball back and forth with you, swinging in the park, paddling in the pool, running an obstacle course, or throwing rocks in a pond. Help her learn eye-hand coordination by blowing bubbles while she chases them and pops them with her index finger. When you take her for a walk in her stroller, alternate stroller riding with walking. Buy her miniature bats, balls, or golf clubs, or make some pins out of potato chip cans and practice bowling. With Dad as a role model, your child will build good fitness habits right from the beginning.

My baby used to be cuddly, but now she frequently pushes me away. Is this normal?

Yes. As babies grow into toddlerhood and learn to crawl and then walk, they become more independent physically—and that translates into greater emotional independence as well. Your child isn't rejecting you; instead, she's developing self-confidence and asserting her independence.

Afterword

"Dad's My Hero"

When did you become a hero? It started the day your partner said, "I'm pregnant," and you hugged her and said, "That's wonderful! I love you!"—even though a little part of you was absolutely terrified at the prospect of adding a baby to your life. You earned more "hero points" when you spent long hours after work at Lamaze class, consoled your partner as her feet swelled and her zippers split, and let her cry on your shoulder when her hormones did their crazy pregnancy dance. Then there was the day you made it through the labor and delivery like a trooper, and were rewarded a thousand times over by your first gaze into the penetrating, unblinking eyes of the newborn who stole your heart.

By now, your child is a toddler, and you're an experienced parent. You've survived colic, poopy diapers, crying jags, spit-up, and teething. However, your job as a parent is only beginning.

As your baby turns into a toddler, a child, a teenager, and eventually a young adult, you'll still be needed every day. That's because for the rest of your child's life, you'll be his most influential male role model. It's no exaggeration to say that even if you never fly a fighter plane, save a life, or win a Super Bowl, you have the opportunity to be your child's greatest hero.

Why? Because the most important man your child will ever know is you. If your child is a boy, he'll spend much of his life striving to be just like you. If your child is a girl, she's likely to seek a life partner who reminds her of you. Who you are and how you behave will define, in your child's mind, what an Ideal Man should and shouldn't do.

It's an awesome responsibility, and you won't always be able to fulfill it. Sometimes you'll screw up. Sometimes you'll fall short. Frequently you'll yell when you should listen. Sometimes you'll give in when you should stand firm. And once in a while you'll do or say things so spectacularly dumb that you'll expect the Parenting Police to pull you over and revoke your license. In short, you'll never be as perfect as the dads on *Leave It to Beaver* or *Seventh Heaven,* because no real-life dad possibly could be.

But, perfect or not, you'll be one of the most important positive influences in your child's life. Over the next twenty years, you'll pass on an enormous amount of wisdom and experience. You'll show your child, by your actions, how strong, brave, gentle, kind, smart, and loyal an adult can be. You'll show him how to resist the urge to commit foolish or unkind acts, and how to atone when he makes a mess of his life. You'll teach him, by example, how to take the high road when the low road would be easier. You'll impress on him the importance of honoring commitments, standing up for what's right, and caring for his family, his friends, his community, and his planet. You'll teach him the skills he'll need to be competent, and the values he'll need to be honorable.

In addition, you'll be your child's most important mirror. Your child will view himself through your eyes, measuring his accomplishments by your pride and calculating the seriousness of his misdeeds by the depth of your disappointment. He'll judge his own worth largely by what you think of him, and what you say about him. Adults who succeed often credit their fathers—"He believed in me." "He taught me." "He knew I could do it." Conversely, those abandoned or rejected by their fathers are at high risk of lifelong failure; in fact, according to statistics from the National Fatherhood Initiative and the FBI, children abandoned or rejected by their fathers comprise 72 percent of teenage murderers, 60 percent of rapists, 70 percent of criminals, 90 percent of runaways, and three out of four teen suicides. Clearly, how well you do your job as a father over the next two decades can make an enormous difference—even a life-or-death difference—in your child's life.

It's a little frightening to hold so much power over your child's future, and there will be times when you'll wonder whether you're man enough for the job. Fortunately, the rules for being a great father are pretty simple. Here are the most important guidelines for being a Superdad:

1. *Make time for your child.* I know it seems impossible on those days when the boss wants you to put in overtime, the yard needs to be mowed, and the checkbook has to be balanced. But set aside at least fifteen minutes every day to read or play with your child—or, when he's older, to shoot a few baskets while you talk about what's important to him. If you have to short your sleep by a few minutes, it's worth the sacrifice. You'll realize, years from now, that these early days flew by too fast. Make the most of them, because in parenting, how well you use these early plays can determine the outcome of the game.

2. *Tell your child every day that you love him*—and show him, too, with hugs and praise.

3. *Tell your child you will ALWAYS love him,* no matter what happens. All children will do terrible things, at one time or another. They need to know that you'll discipline them when they slip, but they need to know that the father-child bond is too strong to be broken.

4. *Catch your child being good.* Avoid falling into the trap of being the family enforcer, whose only role is to criticize when things go wrong. Instead, look for opportunities to give your child a pat on the back: "I like the way you helped Mommy carry those boxes," or, later on, "Thanks for being a good sport when I said you couldn't take the car—I'm proud of you."

5. *Recognize your child's accomplishments.* Whether it's his first finger painting, his attendance award in first grade, or the slightly singed birthday cake he bakes for you all by himself when he's thirteen, let him know you're impressed. A scribbled picture or a good report

card taped to the refrigerator will mean more to your child than a roomful of expensive toys.

6. *Tell other people you're proud of him, too.* One of the best ways to show your child that you're proud of him is to tell the world—especially when he's listening. Carry a brag book of photos around with you, and show them off at the drop of a hat. When the neighbors stop by, or relatives come to visit, be sure to mention your toddler's latest achievements and funny sayings. When he gets older, display his trophies and school awards prominently, and call up Grandma or Grandpa to wax eloquent about his accomplishments. Even if he looks pained when you brag about him, trust me—he's enjoying it. And you're sending two important messages to him: one is that you're paying attention to what happens in his life, and the other is that you're proud.

7. *Establish daily rituals.* No matter how simple or silly they seem, rituals are a powerful glue that strengthens the bond between you and your child. With a toddler or preschooler, rituals can be as simple as flying your child into bed each night, or singing favorite songs together. As your child gets older, the rituals will evolve and change, but the meaning behind them—the message, "You and I have something special together"—will remain the same.

8. *Be the parent, not the child.* Too often, parents fail to discipline and guide because they're afraid their children won't like them. But parenting isn't a popularity contest. The days when your child needs you most are often the days when he'll like you the least.

9. *Be a gentleman.* Even in the Age of Marilyn Manson, manners count. By watching you, your child will learn how to treat other people with dignity, respect, and courtesy.

Above all, be sure your child knows that your family is a team. You won't always get along, and you won't always be happy—in fact, some days you'll barely be able to stand each other—but your child needs to know that you're in his corner, no matter what. How do you teach him that you can be counted on? If your child has a crisis, be there to support him. If he makes a mistake, no matter how serious, help him find a way to overcome it. If he's sad, comfort him. If he misbehaves, teach him how to act better. If he does something stupid or embarrassing, let him know that you've been there yourself and survived. If he needs advice, offer him the benefit of your experience. If he's hurting from a lost love, a failed class, or football defeat, give him a shoulder to cry on.

You and your child will endure many tests together, because while dads aren't perfect, neither are kids—even the best of them. But if you stand by your child in his struggles, he'll reward you a thousand times over during good times: long days at the ballpark, happy moments laughing at the dinner table, proud days at graduations, and even the day when he proudly introduces you to his own first child. So make it clear to your child that you're proud of him, even when he's not perfect, and do your best to make him proud of you. If you do, you'll be his hero for life—and that's the most important game any dad can win.

Appendix

Baby's Behavior: What to Expect, When, and How to Deal with It

BEHAVIOR	AGE RANGE	STRATEGIES
Doesn't sleep through night/wakes.	Birth–one year	Pat your baby on her back, swaddle her tightly for security and stability, and put her in her bassinet.
Needs to eat during the night.	Birth–6 months	Feed your baby just before putting her to sleep. Try giving her a pacifier. Your baby will need to eat at night for at least the first 8–12 weeks.
Fusses, cries inconsolably, and doesn't respond to attempts to calm her.	Birth	Try walking, rocking, taking a bath together. Try singing your baby's name or a song over and over.
Wants to be held constantly; doesn't calm when being rocked.	Birth–3 weeks	Become aware of your baby's responses to voice, movement, or touch, and provide comfort using your baby's most receptive sensory system.

BEHAVIOR	AGE RANGE	STRATEGIES
Has a limited ability to wait when hungry or upset; requires immediate attention.	Birth–2 months	Provide verbal reassurance: "You're okay."
Begins to soothe herself by sucking her finger, or stroking a surface.	4–8 weeks	Help your baby put her finger or thumb in her mouth, or help her stroke her blanket slowly. Try a pacifier.
Becomes more responsive to facial expressions.	6 weeks–3 months	Calm with vocal reassurance ("You're okay") and patting; say "Good, Hannah."
Spits when fed solids.	4–8 months	Push down on your baby's tongue when feeding her solids. Stroke the top of her lip to help keep food in her mouth. Feed very small amounts ($\frac{1}{4}$ to $\frac{1}{2}$ teaspoon). Say "close mouth."
Pinches, pulls hair, scratches.	4–6 months	Get face-to-face and establish eye contact with your baby. Firmly and gently remove her fingers and say "gentle touch." If she repeats the behavior, say "hurt" and repeat above action.
Screams when learning to make sounds; "plays" with sound.	6–9 months	Get face-to-face with your baby. Say firmly, "soft voice." If she screams again, frown, put your hands over your ears, say "too loud!" and then whisper "indoor voice." Praise her next modulated vocalization.

BEHAVIOR	AGE RANGE	STRATEGIES
Cries when a parent leaves the room.	4–8 months	Say "miss Dad/Mom? I'm here." Talk to her from another room or behind a closed door—"back soon!" Give her a soft toy or blanket to hold.
Cries when a stranger wants to hold her.	4–8 months	Don't force this; your baby will probably become more comfortable around strangers at 9–12 months. Show her pictures of friends/relatives so she can become familiar with them.
Short attention span (1–2 minutes).	4–6 months	Read short books and play repetitive games to help your baby build attention span and focus. Encourage your child to look at pictures in books and "eye point"—e.g., "Where is the dog?"
Throws toys.	6–9 months	Establish eye contact. Say, "toys stay here," and tap area where your baby is playing to provide visual and auditory prompts. If she continues to throw the toys, say, "Bye-bye, toys," and put them up where she can see them but they're out of reach.
Hits unintentionally.	4–8 months	Establish eye contact. Say "gentle touch." If she hits again, establish eye contact and say "hurt" and make a sad face. Say "gentle touch" and demonstrate.

BEHAVIOR	AGE RANGE	STRATEGIES
Bangs on table with a toy.	6–10 months	Say "quiet toy." Hold your baby's hand and demonstrate how to play with the toy. Praise when she stops banging—"Good job playing with toy."
Can wait 1–3 minutes/ calms herself or calms to parent's voice.	3–6 months	Praise your baby when she waits well or calms herself.
Touches objects when told no.	6 months and upward	Try to put objects you don't want your baby to touch out of reach. Redirect by handing her a toy she enjoys. If she persists, say, "Not for baby." Try giving her a sock or small towel so she can play "tug-of-war" with you.
Responds inconsistently to commands such as "stop."	6 months and upward	Say "stop" and try redirecting with a toy or activity. Restrain your baby physically. Pick her up and remove her from the situation.
Grabs electrical cords, tries to pull or chew on them.	5–9 months	Say "stop" and try to redirect with another toy or activity. Enclose cords in plastic tubing or cord holders when possible. Give your baby rubber links, toy key chain, etc., as substitutes. Physically restrain and remove from situation to swing, Exersaucer, or another room.

BEHAVIOR	AGE RANGE	STRATEGIES
When fed, grabs for spoon.	5–8 months	Give your baby her own spoon to hold. Give her finger foods (Cheerios, $1/4$ graham cracker) so she can participate.
Throws finger foods, turns her bowl upside down, tosses her Tippee cup, rubs food in her hair or on high chair tray.	5–9 months	Offer only small amounts of food (1–2 Cheerios). Give your baby a toy or spoon to occupy her hands. If she tosses her bowl, say "all done," remove her from her high chair, and don't feed her for at least an hour.
Doesn't want to use a spoon.	4–9 months	Hold your baby's hand on the spoon and scoop together, using a food such as yogurt that is hard to eat with fingers. Try only 1–3 bites at a time, using a spoon with a large, easy-to-hold rounded handle and praising successes. Together with your baby, practice feeding a stuffed animal or doll with a spoon—or let her practice feeding you.
Cries when put down for a nap/bedtime.	6 months and upward	Prepare your baby for this transition by cuddling her closely and reading a story or singing a song. When you put her in her crib, continue to touch her for a minute or so.

BEHAVIOR	AGE RANGE	STRATEGIES
Grabs any object within reach/responds inconsistently to the command "give me the book."	4–8 months	Hold out your hand and request "give me the book," keeping your child physically focused and restrained and waiting for a response. If she needs an additional prompt, remove the object. Practice giving/receiving/exchanging toys.
Climbs on tables, counters, or window sills.	8 months and upward	Say "sit on bottom," physically prompt. Say "danger" and redirect to another activity or toy. Provide outlets (cardboard box, small hassock, indoor slide, etc.) for climbing urge. Visit the park and let your child climb safely on the playground equipment.
Hears command "stop," looks at parent, but continues behavior.	6–9 months	Immediately physically restrain child to reinforce the meaning of the word "stop." Praise child for responding to "stop" by smiling, patting her back, and saying "good listening."
Tries to push buttons on the VCR, TV, stereo, or telephone.	8 months and upward	Place objects up high out of reach wherever possible. Physically redirect to another toy or activity. Substitute child-size toy remote, cell phone, CD player. Get VCR cover/lock.
Takes remote, keys, or other objects, and doesn't want to give them back.	8 months and upward	Physically remove object by trading for another toy.

BEHAVIOR	AGE RANGE	STRATEGIES
Sometimes responds to "stop"; other times smiles and ignores you, and continues the behavior.	10 months and upward	Establish eye contact, speak in a firm voice, physically restrain if necessary, redirect. Expect response within one minute and with only one warning. Praise independent response by saying "good stopping" or "good listening."
Takes things off shelves or out of cupboards or drawers.	8 months and upward	Give your child her own cupboard or drawer; change contents from time to time to keep it interesting. Redirect when she gets into your things, say "stop" or physically remove if necessary.
Dumps out contents of your wallet or briefcase, or messes with the papers on your desk.	9 months and upward	Keep your wallet and briefcase out of reach. Expect a baby of this age to explore anything at eye level or below.
Pulls or pushes the dog or cat.	9 months and upward	Say "hurts." Say "gentle touch" and demonstrate by gently petting the animal. Keep your child away from pets when you can't supervise them.
Grabs a toy object from someone else.	9 months and upward	Give your child another toy, and hand back the one that was taken. Say "John's toy. Here's your toy." Children this age do not share or understand ownership.

BEHAVIOR	AGE RANGE	STRATEGIES
Lacks understanding of ownership.	9 months and upward	Build block towers together—one block for dad, one block for baby—and practice knocking them over. Read a story as your child turns the pages.
Attention span of 5–6 minutes (maximum), depending on interest.	9 months	Play games that take 5–10 minutes, to improve attention span (for instance, build a road of blocks and play with cars on it).
Is noisy in church or in a restaurant.	6 months and upward	It's unrealistic to expect a child of this age to be quiet; hire a baby-sitter if a social situation requires quiet behavior.
Has difficulty sitting still in public.	9 months and upward	Children usually can't be expected to sit still in public for more than 15–20 minutes. If possible, take turns with your partner taking your child outside for a "move around" break.
Unaware of danger; tries to step off stairs or top of slide.	9 months and upward	Provide close supervision to prevent injury. Redirect when possible. Say "danger," but don't expect child to understand at first.
Scribbles or colors on the walls or furniture.	9 months and upward	Keep crayons and markers out of reach unless your child is supervised. Buy only washable markers.

BEHAVIOR	AGE RANGE	STRATEGIES
Bites.	9 months and upward	Establish eye contact and say in a firm voice, "hurts," and "no biting." Place your child in time-out, holding her for one minute. Avoid eye contact during time-out. Repeat as needed. Give your child rubber teething toys so you can redirect her.

Acknowledgments

With my deepest gratitude to Cappy Rothman, M.D., Quinton Van der Werf, M.D., and David Hill, M.D.

Thanks also to Julie Chi for wonderful photos, and for seeing the book through to completion.

Many thanks to George Lucas, my editor at Pocket Books, who believed in this book and provided enthusiasm, sensitivity, and outstanding editing.

To Margot Maley Hutchison, Wendy Lind, and Alison Blake, my appreciation for your help.

My admiration and thanks to all the wonderful dads and moms who made time to be photographed and share their beautiful babies and the special times they enjoy together.

Index